Trevor Haddrell

Bristol and Beyond

Bristol and Beyond

Fifty-five Relief Engravings

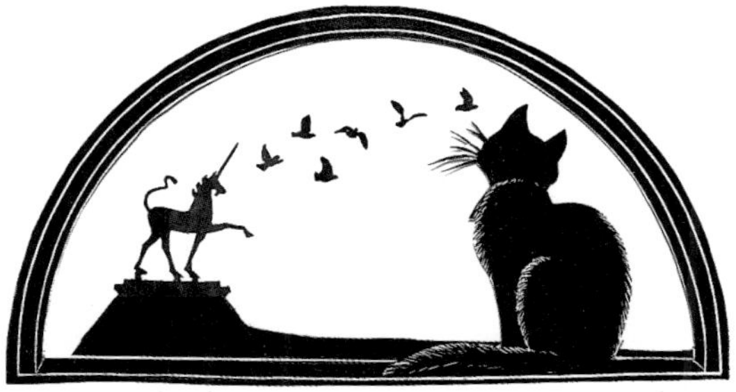

TREVOR HADDRELL

redcliffe

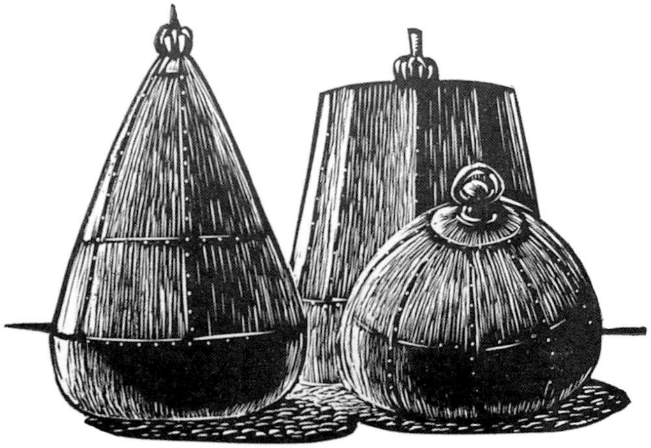

First published in 2006 by Redcliffe Press Ltd.
81g Pembroke Road, Bristol BS8 3EA
0117 973 7207
www.redcliffepress.co.uk

ISBN 10 1 904537 61 8
ISBN 13 9781904537 61 8

British Library Cataloguing-in-Publication Data.
A catalogue record for this book is available from the British Library.

Typeset and designed by Stephen Morris Communications, smc@freeuk.com
and printed by HSW Print (01443) 441100

Contents

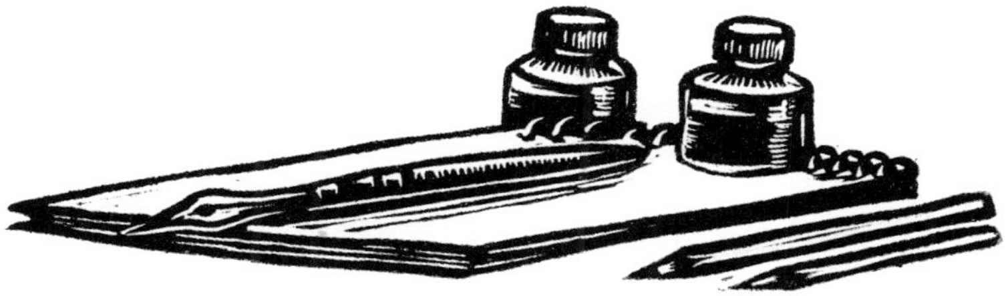

Foreword

It is a great pleasure to be publishing our third book with Trevor Haddrell in the space of four years.

When I invited Trevor to consider undertaking 50 relief engravings of Bristol for publication in book form, I was confident the book would be well received. So popular did that first venture prove that we shall soon have to contemplate a reprint of *Panoramic Bristol*, and we have since published a very different collection – of plant forms – in the beautiful *Asparagus and Other Friends*.

Painter and print-maker Trevor Haddrell hails from Rotherham, but has lived, taught and practised as an artist in Bristol for forty years. After training as an art and design teacher at Bath Academy of Art, Corsham, he taught art at Ashton Park School and at Clifton High School, as Head of Art and Design, before retiring from teaching in 2000. He has since devoted himself to art. If he were not a modest man, Trevor could claim to be one of Bristol's most popular artists. His engravings sell out at venues through the city; his work is in the collections of Bristol Museum & Art Gallery and the Theatre Collection of Bristol University, and has won prizes at the Royal West of England Academy. He is also a full member of the Society of Wood Engravers, where he has been dubbed 'the Chardin of the vegetable world' for his elegant plant engravings.

Invited to be Artist-in-Residence at Bristol Record Office in 2005, Trevor embarked on his largest work ever – an 8-foot panorama stretching from the Suspension Bridge, along the Clifton and Clifton Wood hillsides and taking in the Floating Harbour. Another large panorama, taking in the view from Zero Degrees towards Colston Street, was awarded the St Cuthbert's Mill prize for 'most outstanding work on paper' at that year's RWA annual exhibition.

Since turning full-time professional artist, Trevor feels he is 'a driven man … The days aren't long enough to do all I want to do. I look at drawings I did thirty or even forty years ago, and realise that, without my knowing it at the time, they were really preparatory drawings for engravings – some of the plates in this book are evidence of this.'

With this new set of familiar and not-so-familiar views, Trevor has now completed more than 100 engravings of Bristol, adding up to a unique archive of how the city looks in the early years of the twenty-first century.

John Sansom August 2006

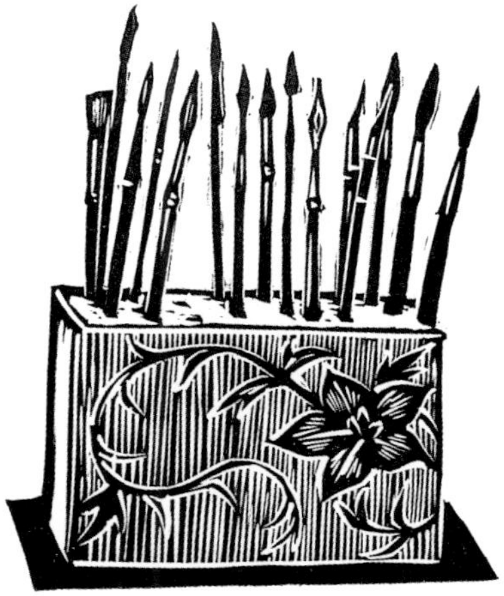

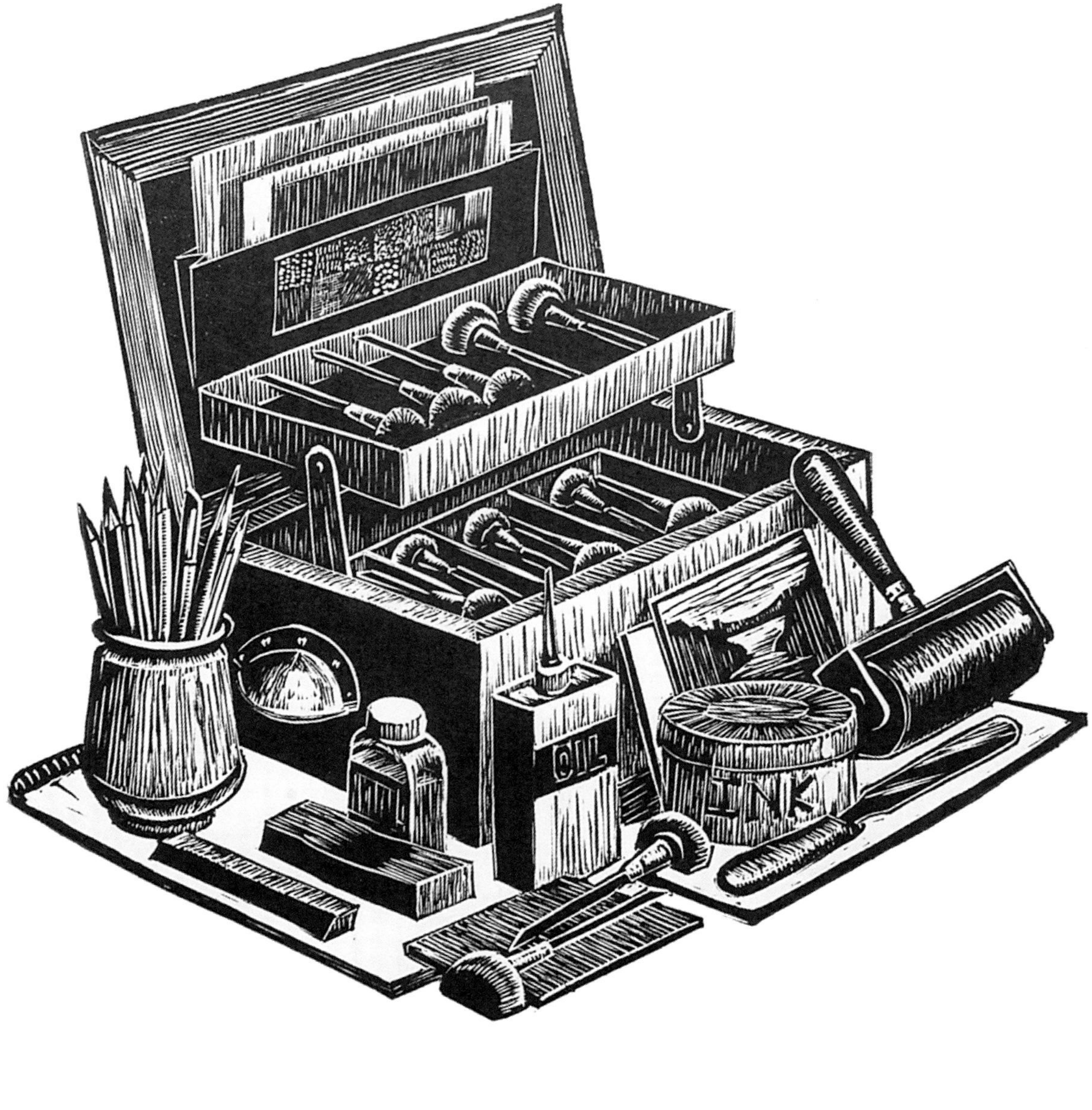
OIL
INK

Artist's Introduction

It is now four years since my first collection of 50 engravings was published under the title of 'Panoramic Bristol'.

Even before that book was on the shelves, I had already completed further engravings of the city and I have continued to add to them each year, culminating in an absolute orgy of production this year when I was determined to have at least another 50 ready for this book, including the largest print I have ever attempted.

Throughout the time I worked on this project I never felt short of ideas for subjects but I had to call a halt when my publisher's deadline approached. I know there is still much I've not even begun to approach in my work on the city. Several good suggestions came to me from people who obtained the first book. I must apologise to them if I've not found time to include their subjects here. I hope to get round to them eventually. (Volume III, perhaps?)

This present collection is loosely divided into five sections:

Around the Docks

Around the City Centre

Clifton, Clifton Wood and Redland

A Theatrical Interlude

and a 'Beyond' section where I have recorded just a few of the places of interest in the vicinity of the city.

Most of these studies are completely new subjects but, in some cases, I have returned to vantage points I adopted for prints in 'Panoramic Bristol' and made an updated version of the view or done a variation on the earlier composition. I never feel I have said the last word, or drawn the final line, about any subject. There's no greater thrill than being surprised by the familiar.

The city is changing rapidly and there are some impressive developments in among the depressingly mediocre. In these works, I have tried either to incorporate the new, or turn a tactful blind eye, as seemed appropriate.

I have lived here for almost 40 years now, and love the city more and more. There is much that is worth recording and celebrating in it. While-ever my eyes and hands are still functioning, I suspect I'll still be producing artwork in response to it.

Trevor Haddrell

August 2006

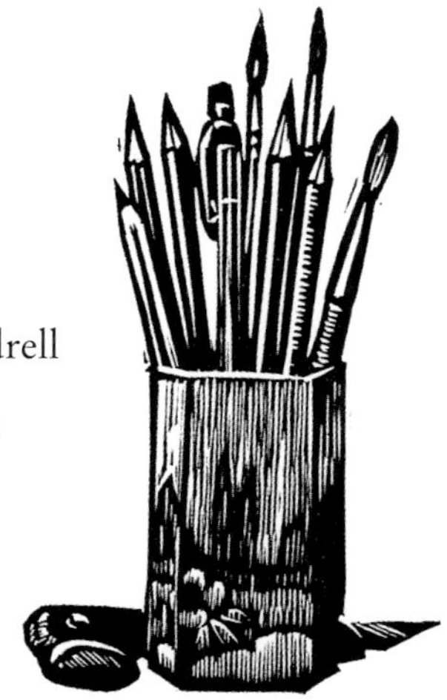

Technique

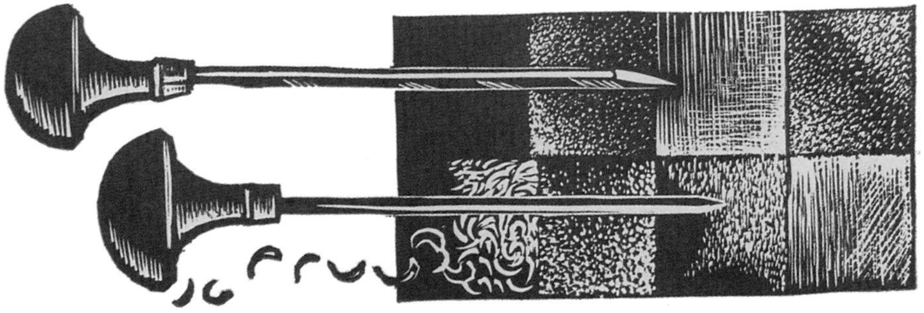

The method I use to produce these engravings is a relief-printing process similar to that used for wood-engraving. Anyone who ever made a lino-cut at school will understand the method because it is simply a more refined version of the one they used.

My designs are based on drawings done from direct observation. I also take many photographs and refer to them often once I have the design drawn out but I feel the experience of sitting in front of the subject and attempting to make an interpretation of it in line and tone is a very important one – only once I've really 'inhabited' a scene in this way can I feel at liberty to play creatively with the information so gained.

And I do play with it: I can stretch and twist perspective in order to manipulate a subject into a satisfactory abstract design and I can decide whether to supply extreme detail or ignore it altogether. The engraved marks I make can vary from tiny and meticulous to bold and expressive. There is no formula: each subject needs an individual response.

Once I have my drawing ready, I trace it and then transfer it, reversed, onto a vinyl block. This is ordinary, 2mm thick commercial flooring vinyl: an absolutely smooth type, as used in schools and offices, preferably in a neutral mid-grey colour. I buy it on the roll and cut off pieces as needed. I pour boiling water over the blocks once they are trimmed to size to remove the curl they acquire on the roll. I coat the surface with thin acrylic gesso so the transferred pencil lines are clear and can be fixed with a black felt-tipped pen.

A mixture of fine lino-cutting and traditional wood-engraving tools is then used to engrave the design.

Whatever is cut out of the block will appear as an area of white in the final print; whatever is left behind will appear black. Tonal variations can be suggested through the use of fine cross-hatchings or stipplings: if the marks are small enough and closely packed, the eye will read them as an area of grey.

Trial, or proof, prints can be taken at any time by rolling a thin layer of ink on the surface of the block, placing a piece of paper on top and applying pressure to the back either by hand with a wooden spoon, or by using a printing press.

The block may then be worked on further to strengthen high-lights or extend areas of stippling or texture until an effective balance between light and dark is achieved.

Edition standard prints can then be made on high quality acid-free paper.

Original Limited Edition Prints

From each of the finished engraved blocks, I make a fixed number of prints entirely by hand on heavyweight fine art paper of conservation standard (usually Somerset Satin, which is made at St Cuthbert's Mill, near Wells). I use an oil-based ink applied to the block with a roller.

These prints have a pleasing, slightly embossed appearance on the velvety surface of the paper when they come off the press: much more sensuous than a photographic reproduction can ever be.

Each one of these prints is then signed and numbered. Editions are limited as indicated.

As I do all this work myself and never pass it on to professional printers who offer editioning services, I tend to print up about a dozen prints at a time until the edition is used up. Then, no more prints are taken.

By these means, I ensure that each of these impressions is a unique, hand-made artefact.

(I am very precise in my use of the term 'original print'. For a work to qualify as such, the artist, in my opinion, must have been intimately and physically involved in the production of each image by hand – photographically reproduced copies of pre-existing drawings or paintings do not merit the term, even if they are signed by the artist. These are 'signed reproductions', not true 'original prints.')

For all except my largest prints, I usually cut mounts and fix them in the frames, myself. It gives satisfaction to be in charge of the entire process.

I have exhibited examples of my work at several venues around the city and had works selected for the annual exhibitions of the Royal West of England Academy and of the Society of Wood Engravers. I was elected a member of this society in May 2006 (even though I have rarely engraved on wood).

I still haven't quite adjusted to the fact that after all my years as a school-teacher I now have the time to actually try and practise what I preached. The days still aren't long enough but it is a blessing to be able to spend them as I do.

As may be clear throughout the pages of this book, I have become somewhat obsessive about this activity of engraving...

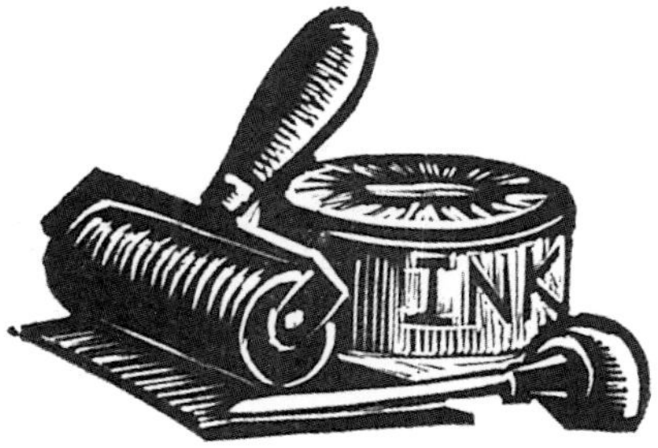

Around the Docks

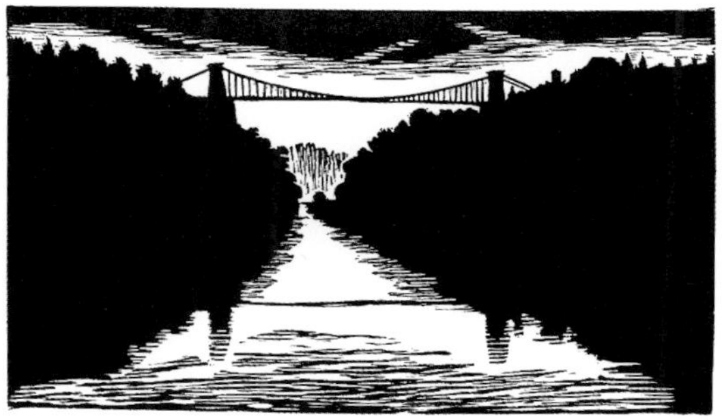

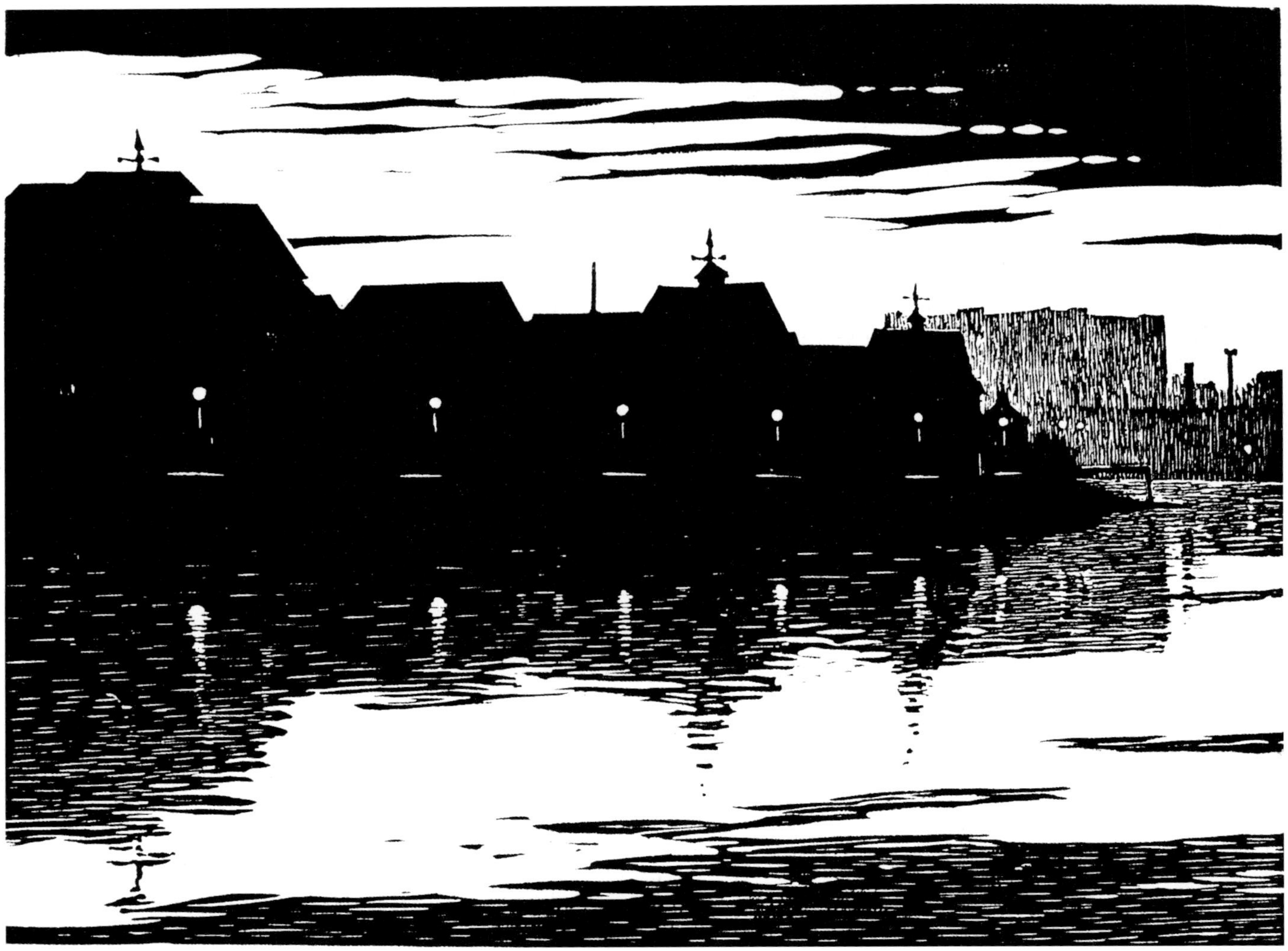

1 *Evening, Baltic Wharf*
actual size

This is the view towards Cumberland Basin near where I live. I've always enjoyed the way that reality and reflections fuse into an abstraction that is surprising and wonderful as the light fades. The next two engravings are variations on this idea.

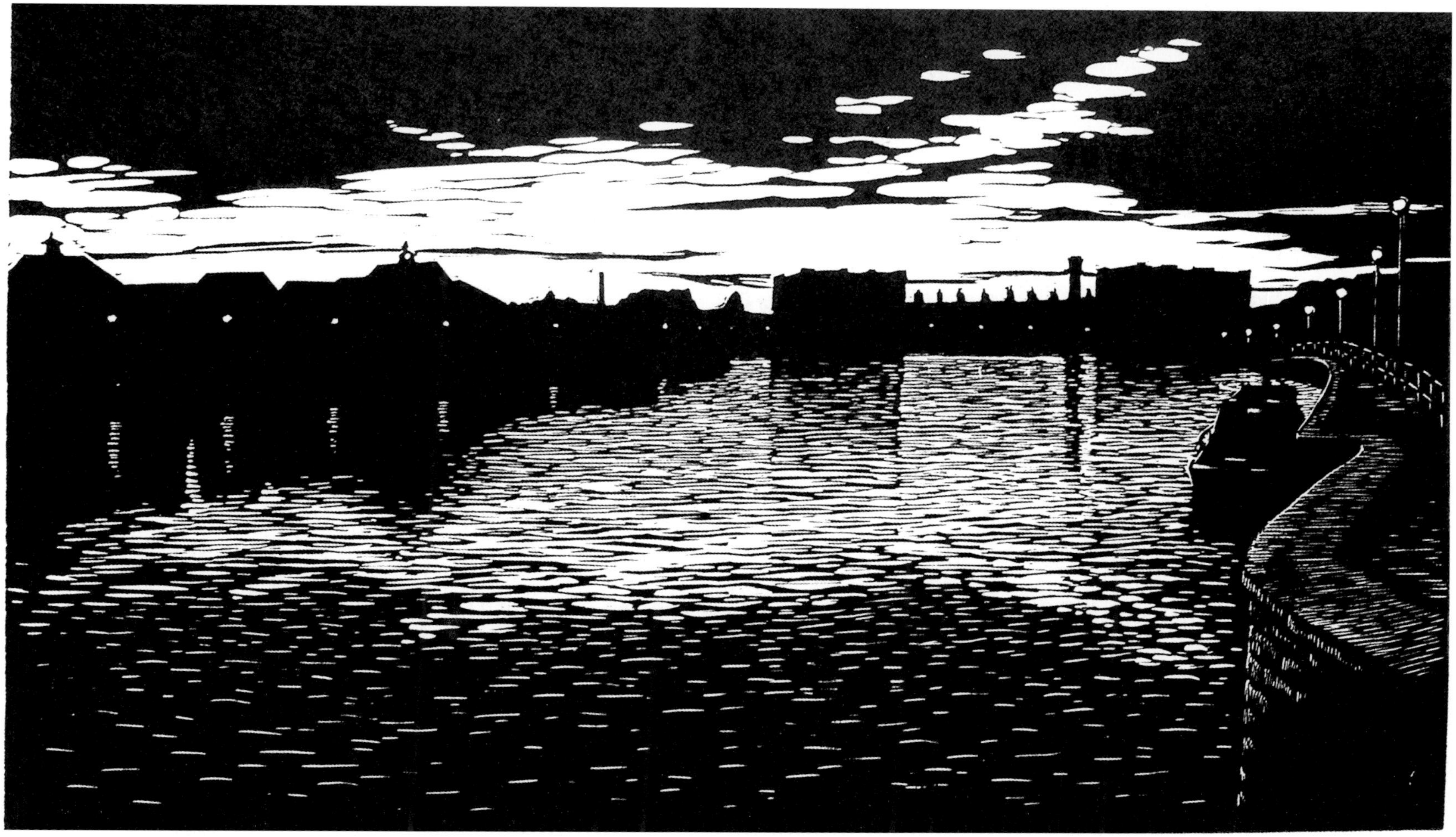

2 *Looking towards Cumberland Basin*
actual size

A little later, with the light fading rapidly, two of the old warehouses are silhouetted in the distance and a continuous band of shapes stretches from left to right, linking the two banks of the Floating Harbour.

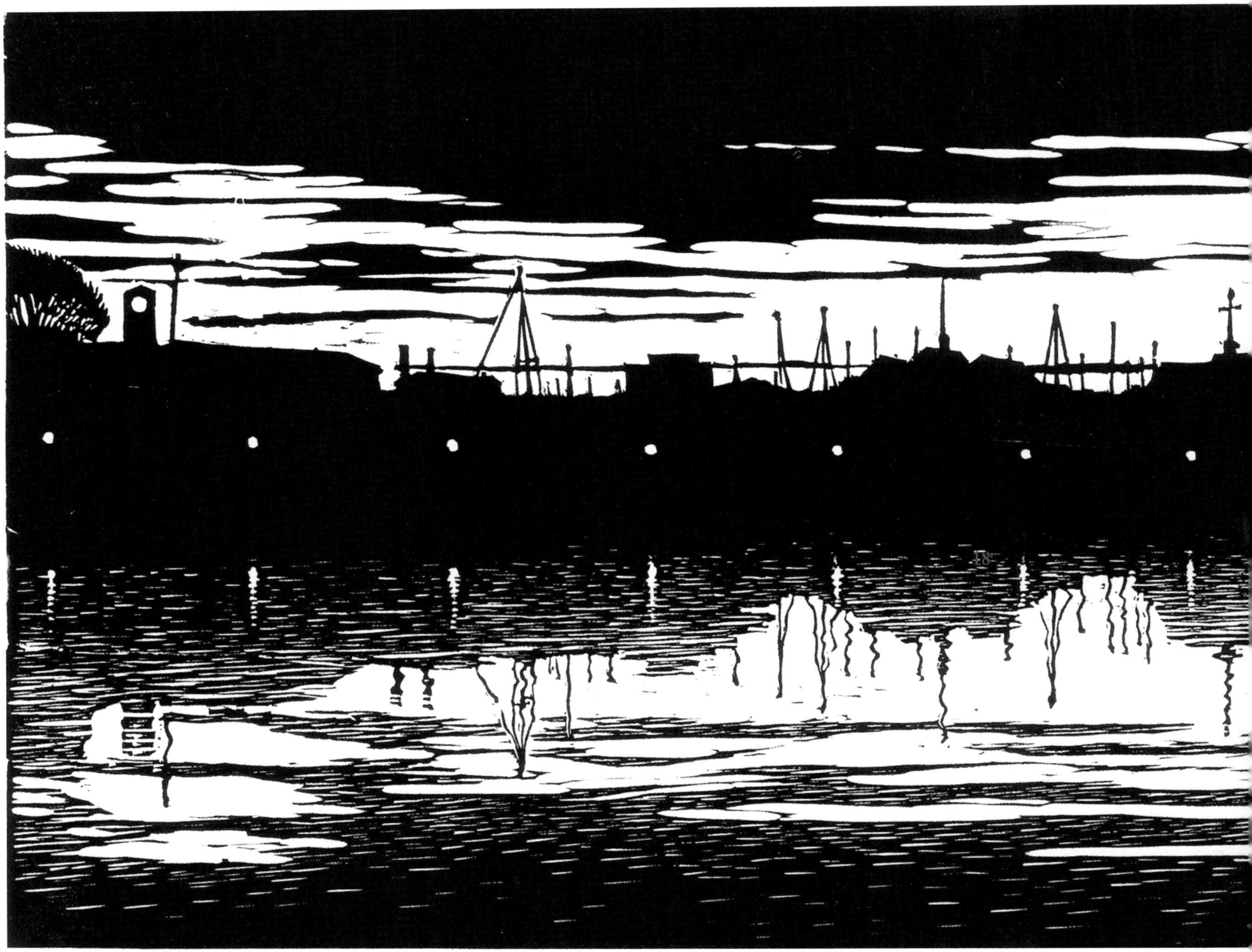

3 *The Marina and Baltic Wharf, looking towards Cumberland Basin*
reduced from 17 x 48cms (7 x 18¾ ins)

This is my most recent engraving. I've striven for absolute economy of mark-making and a simple but expressive abstract design.

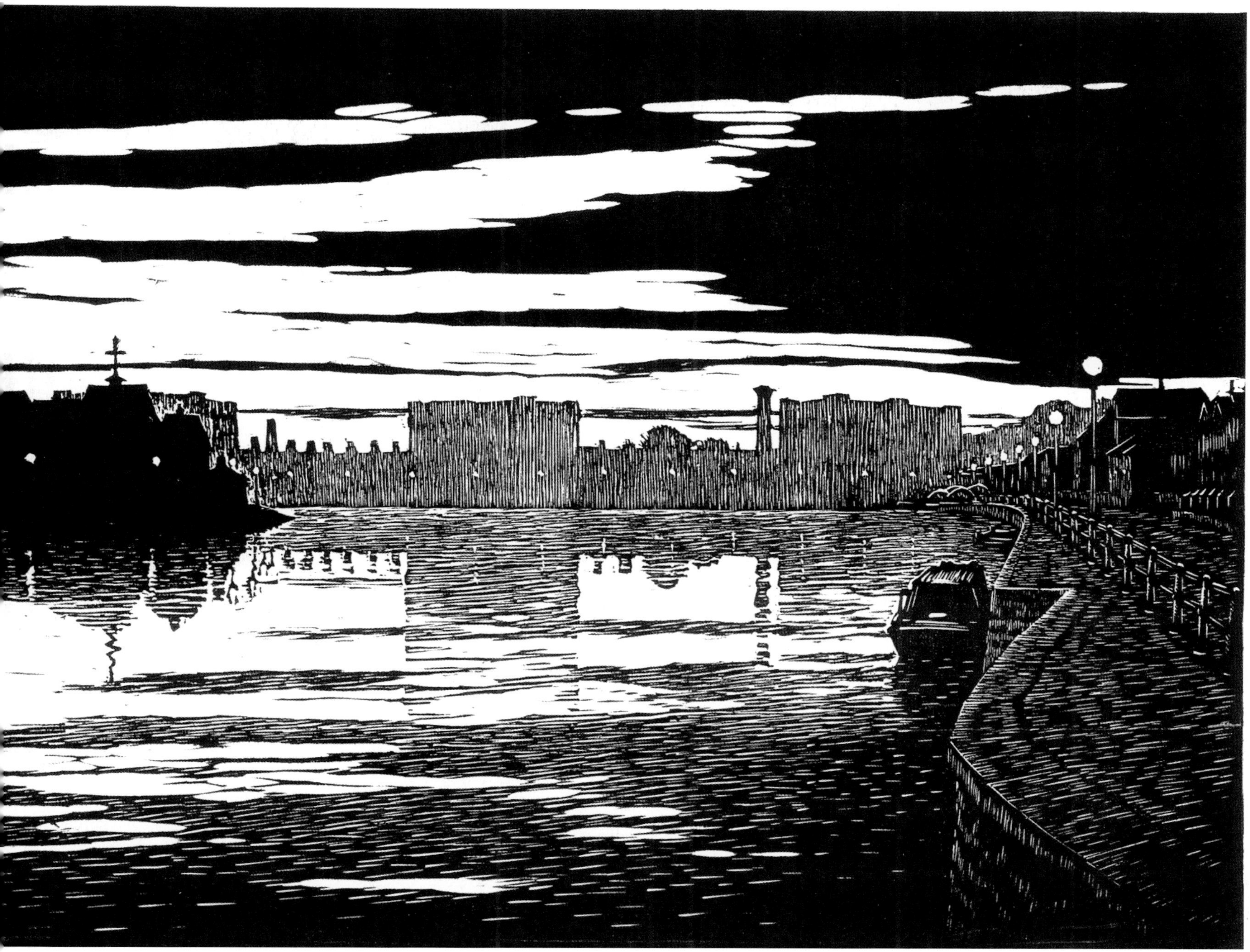

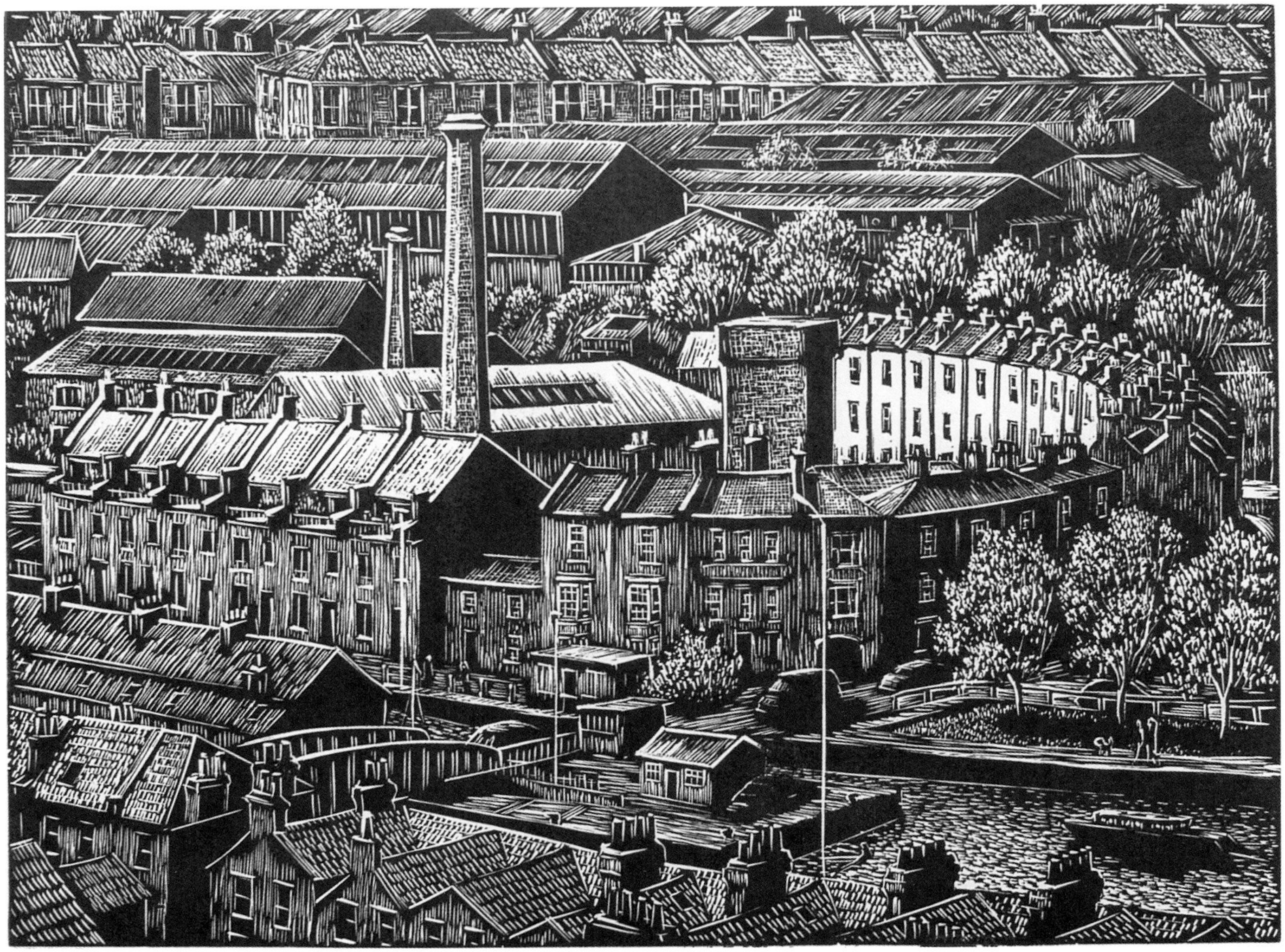

4 *Avon Crescent, Cumberland Basin*
actual size

During 2005, I often walked over the small swing bridge (bottom left) and by the Nova Scotia public house, on my way to the Record Office in 'B' Bond Warehouse where I was Artist-in-Residence.

I drew this scene from the top floor apartment of a friend who lived in Eugenie House up in Clifton.

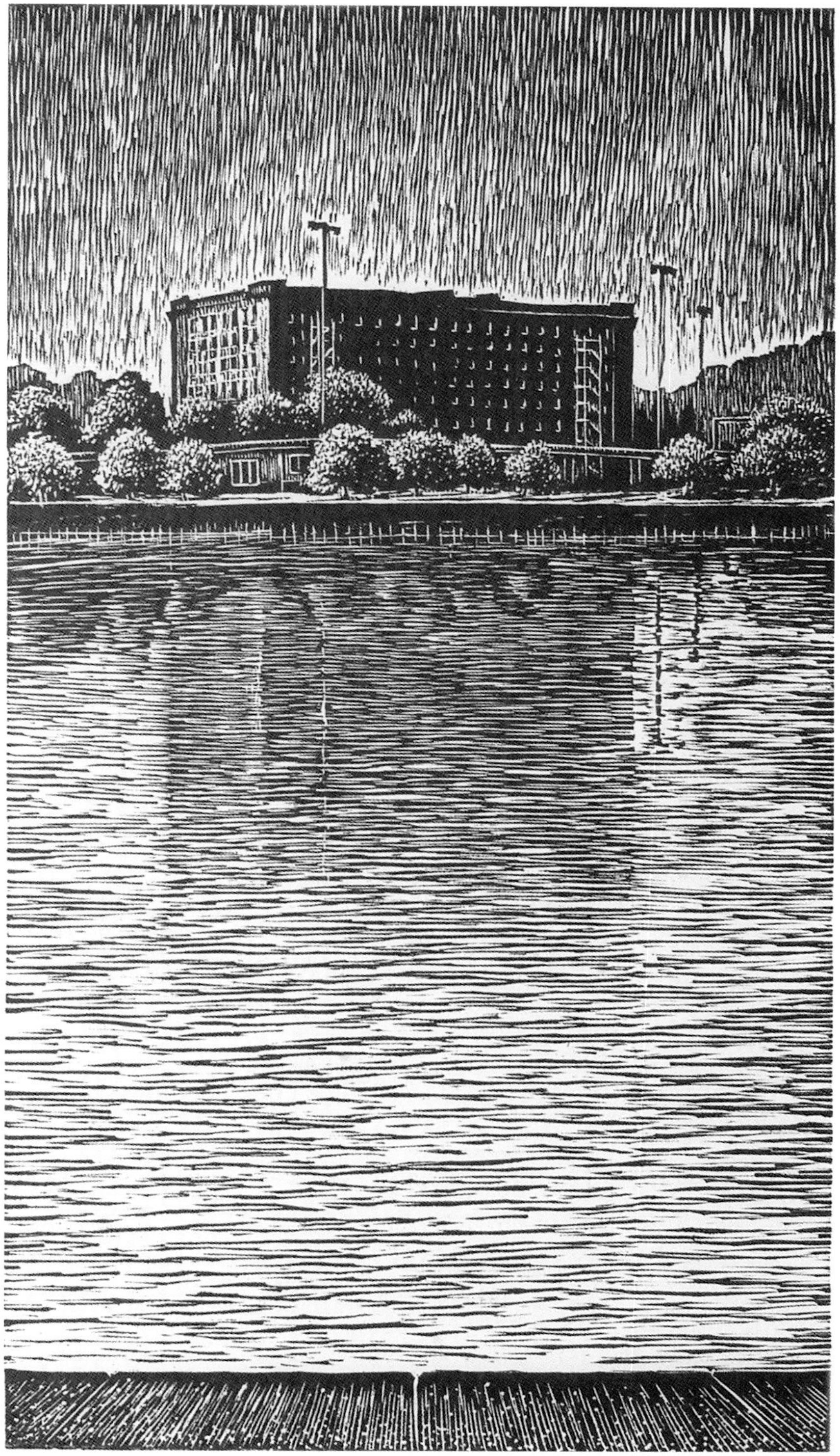

5 *'B' Bond Warehouse, Cumberland Basin*
actual size

In July, 2005, I sat at the top of the external fire escape of this building to sketch the large panorama illustrated next.

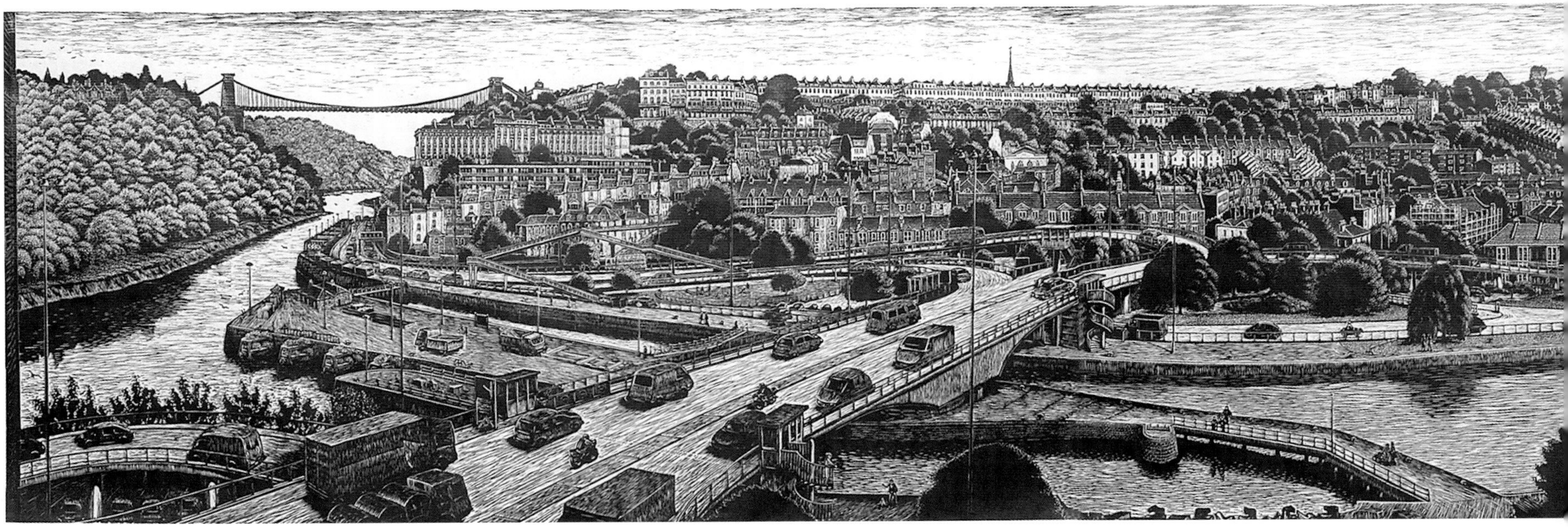

6 *Panorama 'B' Bond, Cumberland Basin*
37 x 250cms (14½ ins x 98½ ins)

In 2005, I was invited to be Artist-in-Residence at the Bristol Record Office situated in 'B' Bond Warehouse.

I suggested I work on a large engraved panorama which I would base on a sketch made from the top of the building. I did this drawing over two weeks in July, sitting at the top of the external fire escape. It was 250cms (8'3") in length when completed and I decided to face up to the challenge it offered and try to produce the engraving exactly the same size as the sketch. This would make it the largest engraving I'd ever attempted.

It would have been too unwieldy to engrave the whole composition on a single block but I discovered it could be divided into three separate sections of 79 x 37cms (31 x 14½ ins). These would each make effective independent compositions but they would also fit together exactly into one continuous design when required.

During my residency at the Record Office, I was able to trace pencil design and then transfer it, reversed, onto the blocks and ink it in with permanent black ink. The actual engraving process then began in December, 2005.

I spent regular 12-hour sessions working on the blocks, sitting with them on my knees and viewing them through a magnifying glass. It took over four months to complete them. (After almost two months work, I completely re-engraved two of the sections on fresh blocks, having grown dissatisfied with my first attempts.)

My main concern throughout the period I was engraving the blocks was to try and keep in mind the large, linking rhythms, running across the panorama, which would bind together the whole composition when viewed from a distance as a single piece.

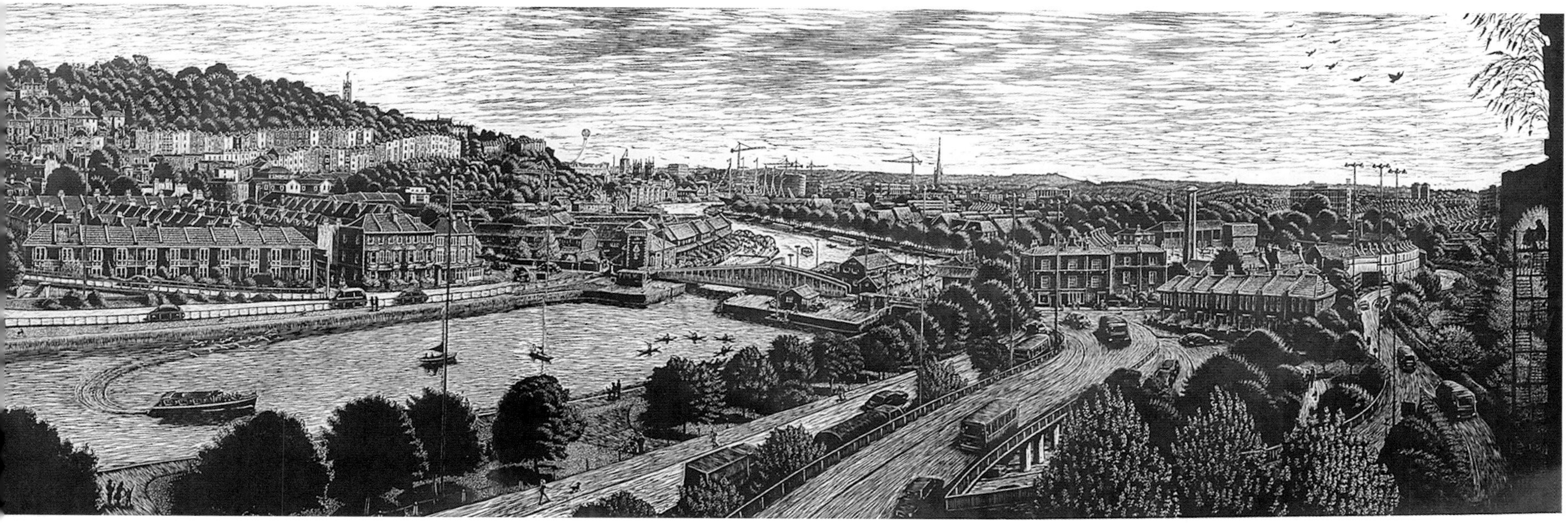

There were also a lot of 'delicious complexities' in the details of this design, of course. I aimed to be as accurate as possible, but I still needed to select what to ignore or simplify and what to emphasise. I decided to try and give as much loving attention to features such as the modern fly-over as I did to Georgian Clifton and the rest of the architecture.

The hope was that by translating the whole of the scene into the language of black-and-white engraving it would give an overall harmony to the subject which might not be quite so apparent in reality.

It was interesting to observe the daily rhythms of life in the scene from my high vantage point – the ebbing and flowing of the Avon under the Suspension Bridge; the regular swings of the large traffic bridge below and smaller events such as the appearance of a children's canoe club in the Floating Harbour on my right and the ferry boats turning just there. Further away, towards the city centre, I could see the many cranes at work on new developments on the harbourside near the ss *Great Britain*, and also the slow rising and falling flights of the tethered air balloon on Castle Park.

It was a real pleasure to work in that spot (though I soon realised my presence upset the local pigeons who were used to landing on a cornice nearby!) – I'd like to return there in the future, if it is possible, to record the scene at different times of the year.

On the following pages are larger reproductions of the three blocks, along with a selection of actual-size details.

The first impression of the print is now on display in the Record Office.

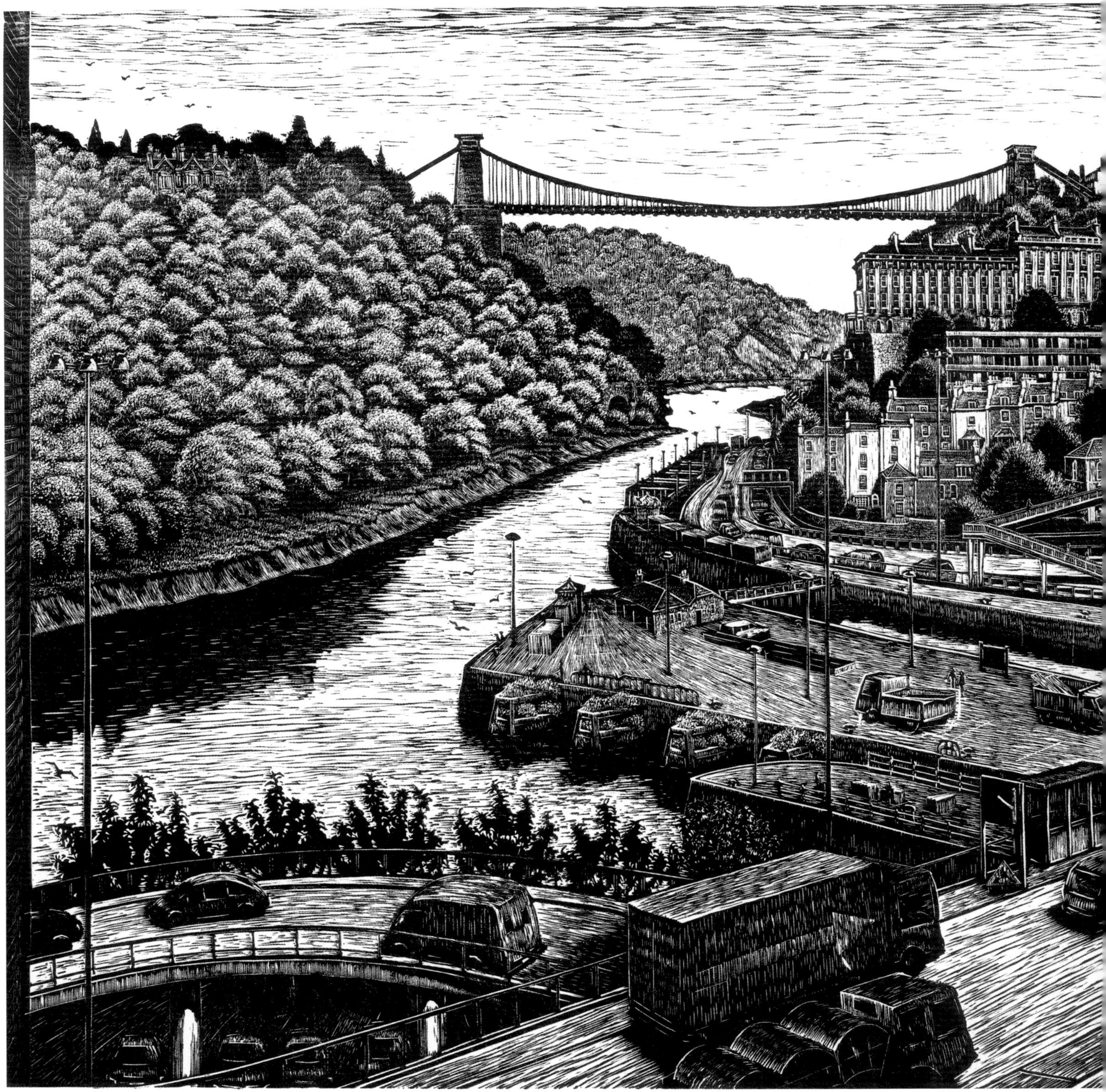

7 *'B' Bond Panorama*
First block
37 x 79cms (14½ x 31ins)

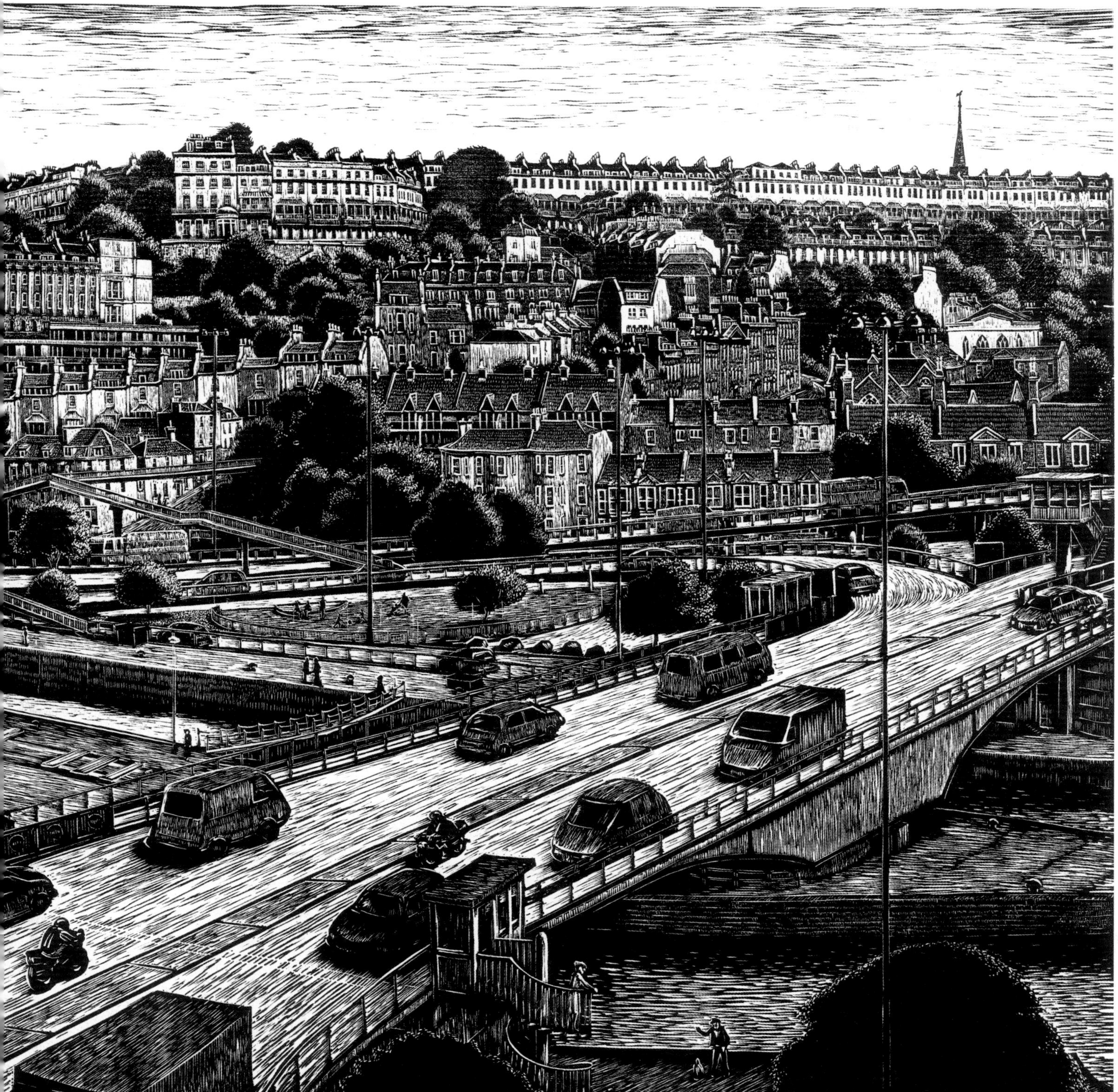

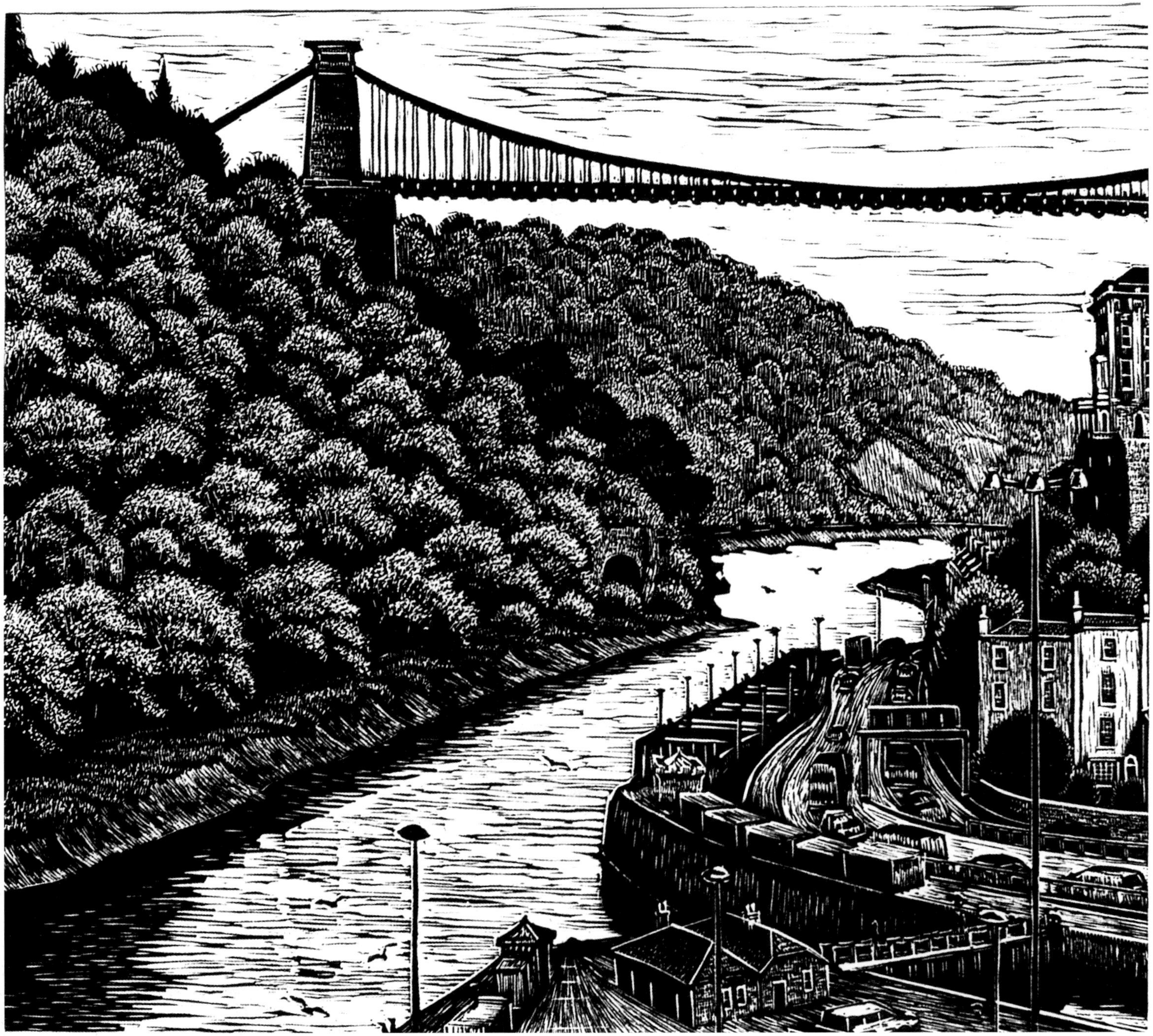

Two actual-size details from the first block.

Part of the Clifton Suspension Bridge.

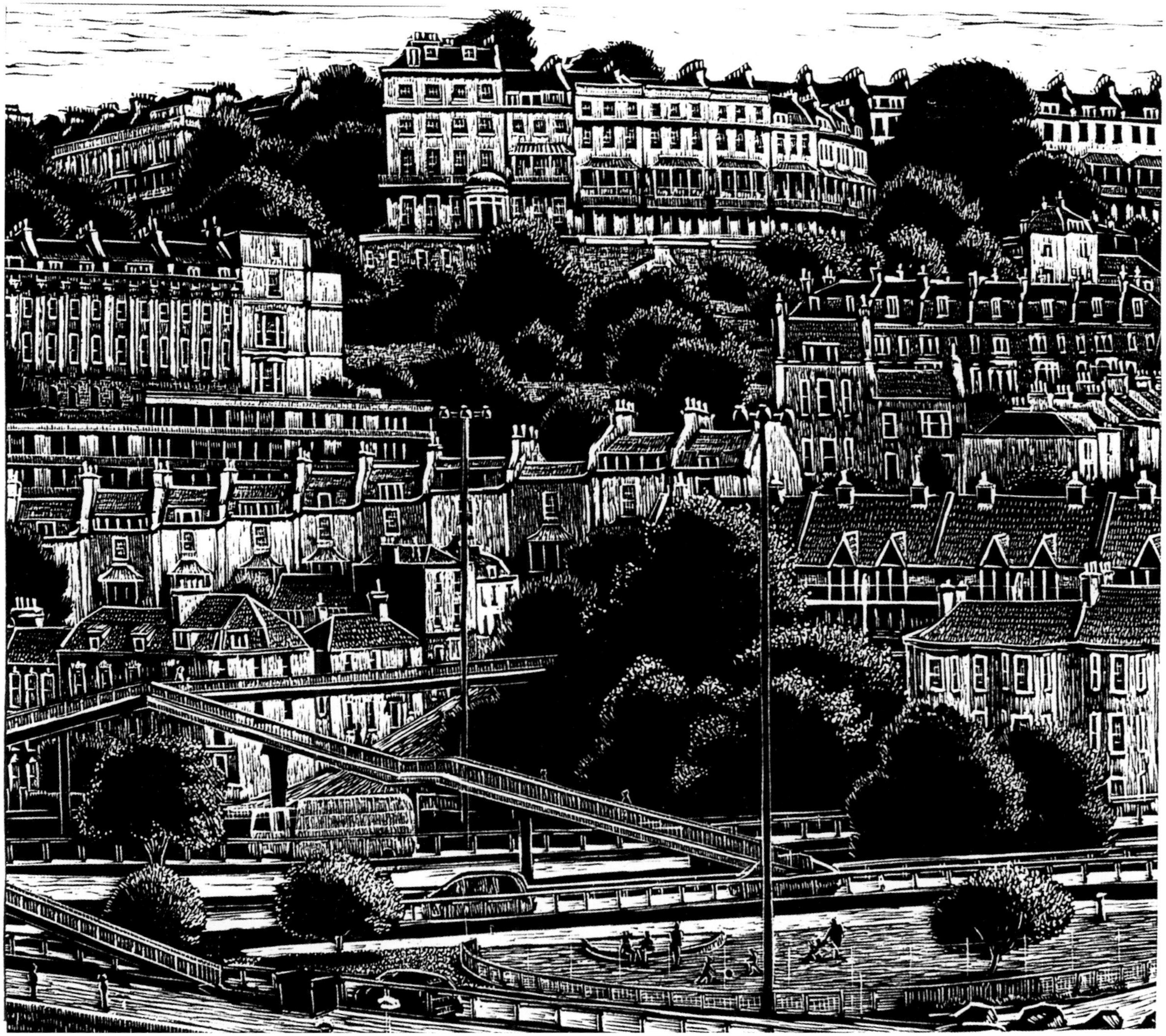

Part of Clifton including the Paragon and the end of Freeland Place below.

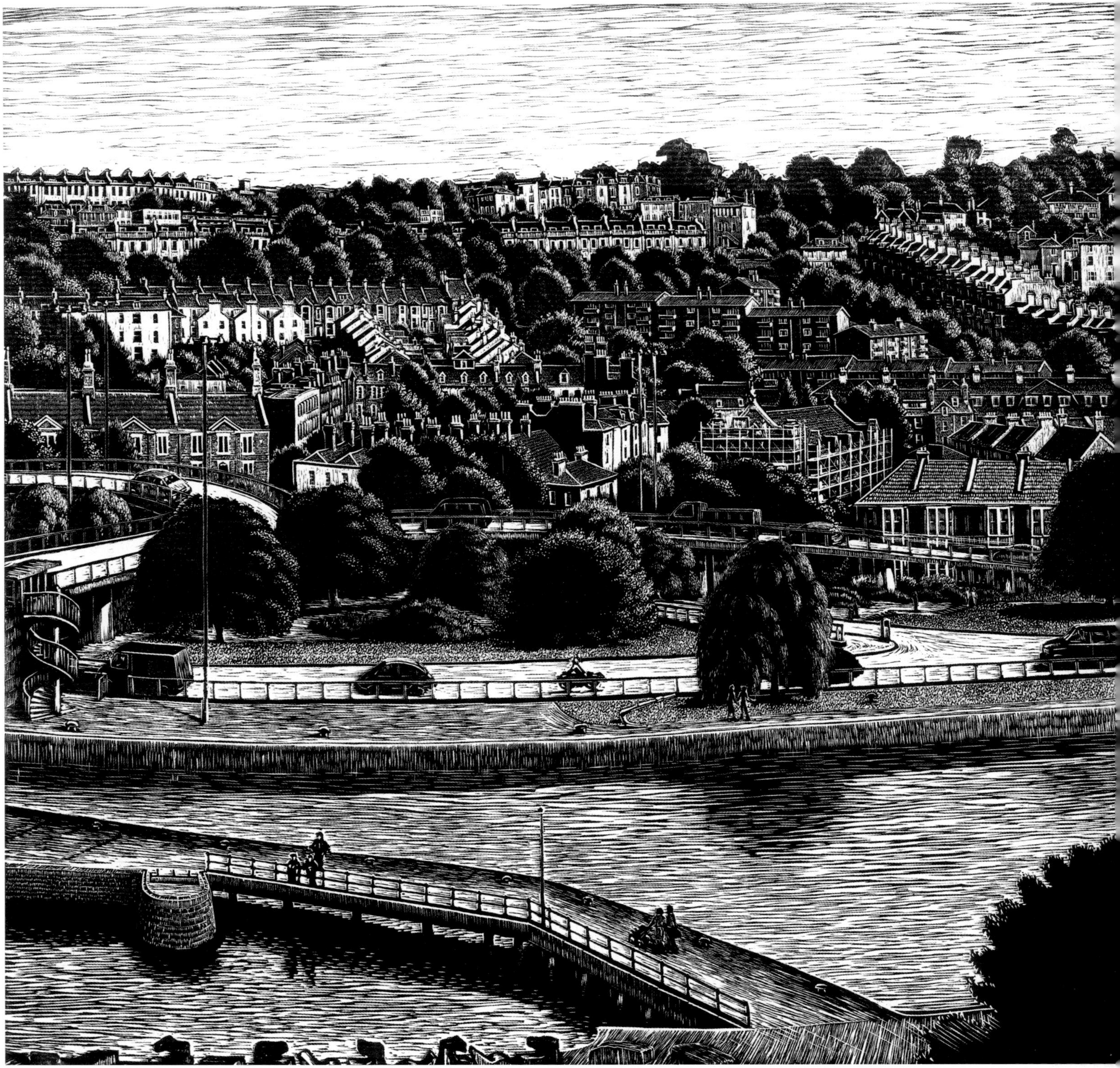

8 *'B' Bond Panorama*
Second block
37 x 79cms (14½ x 31ins)

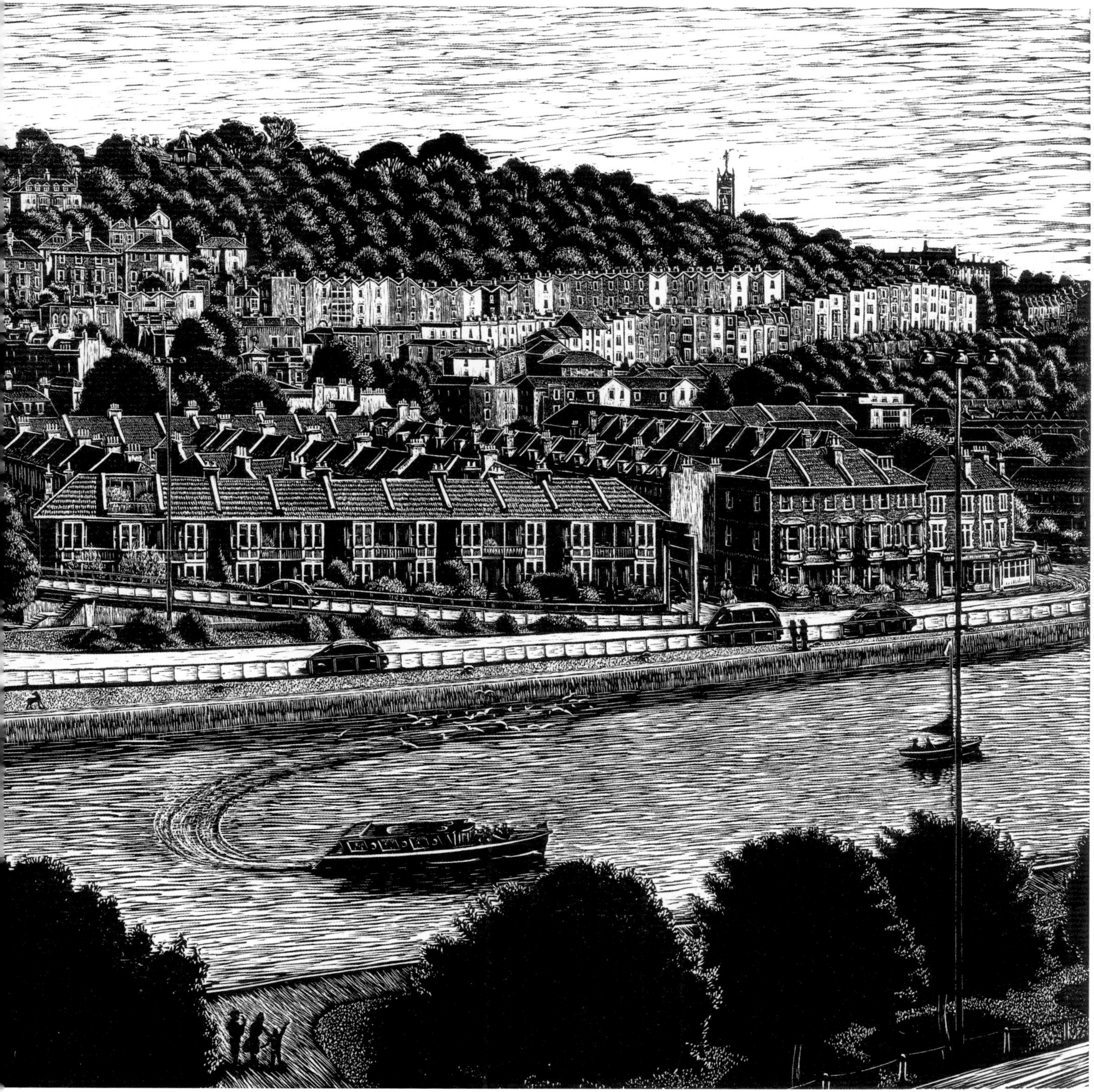

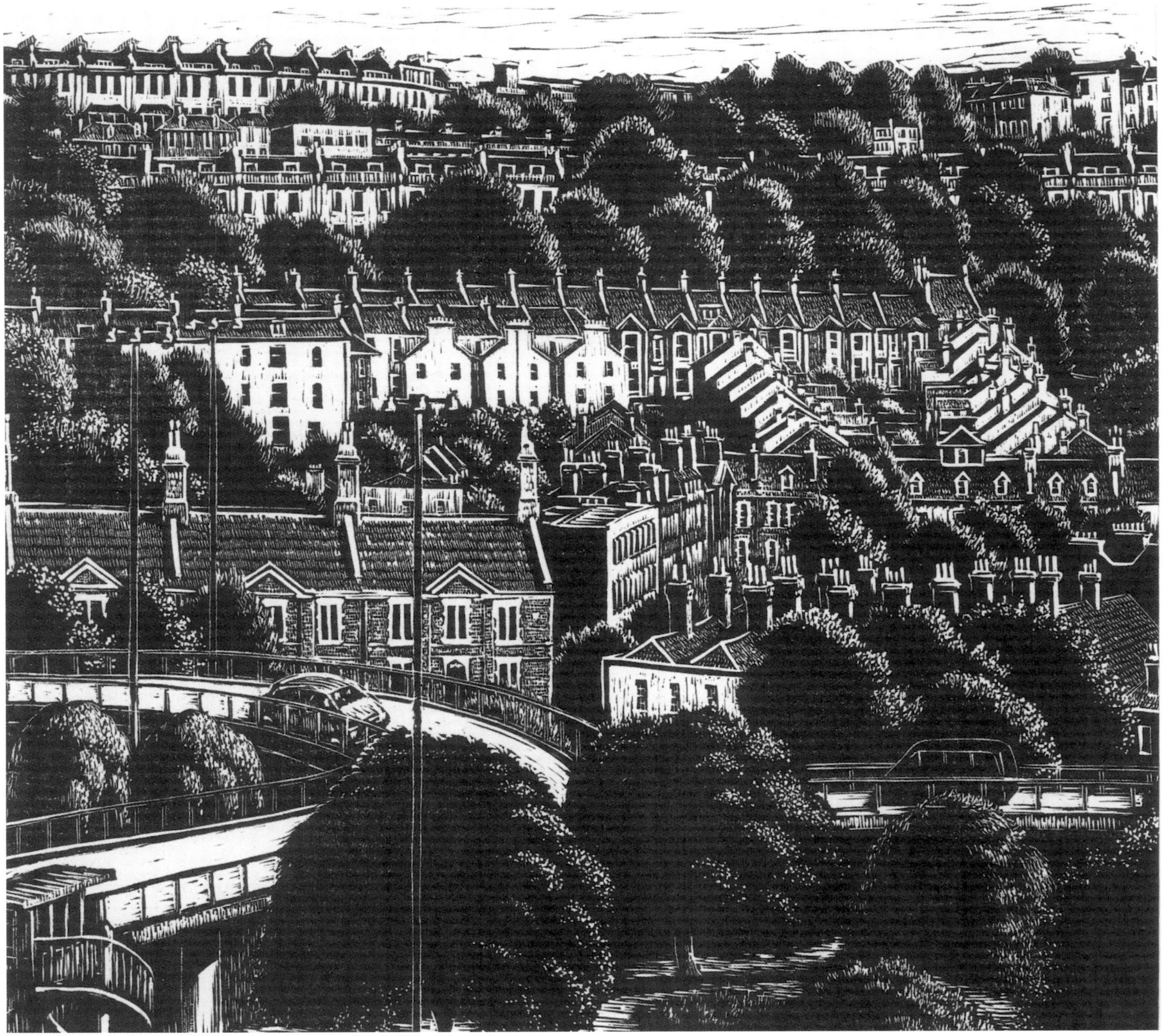

Two actual-size details from the second block.

Looking over Dowry Square (at middle right)
towards Cornwallis Avenue.

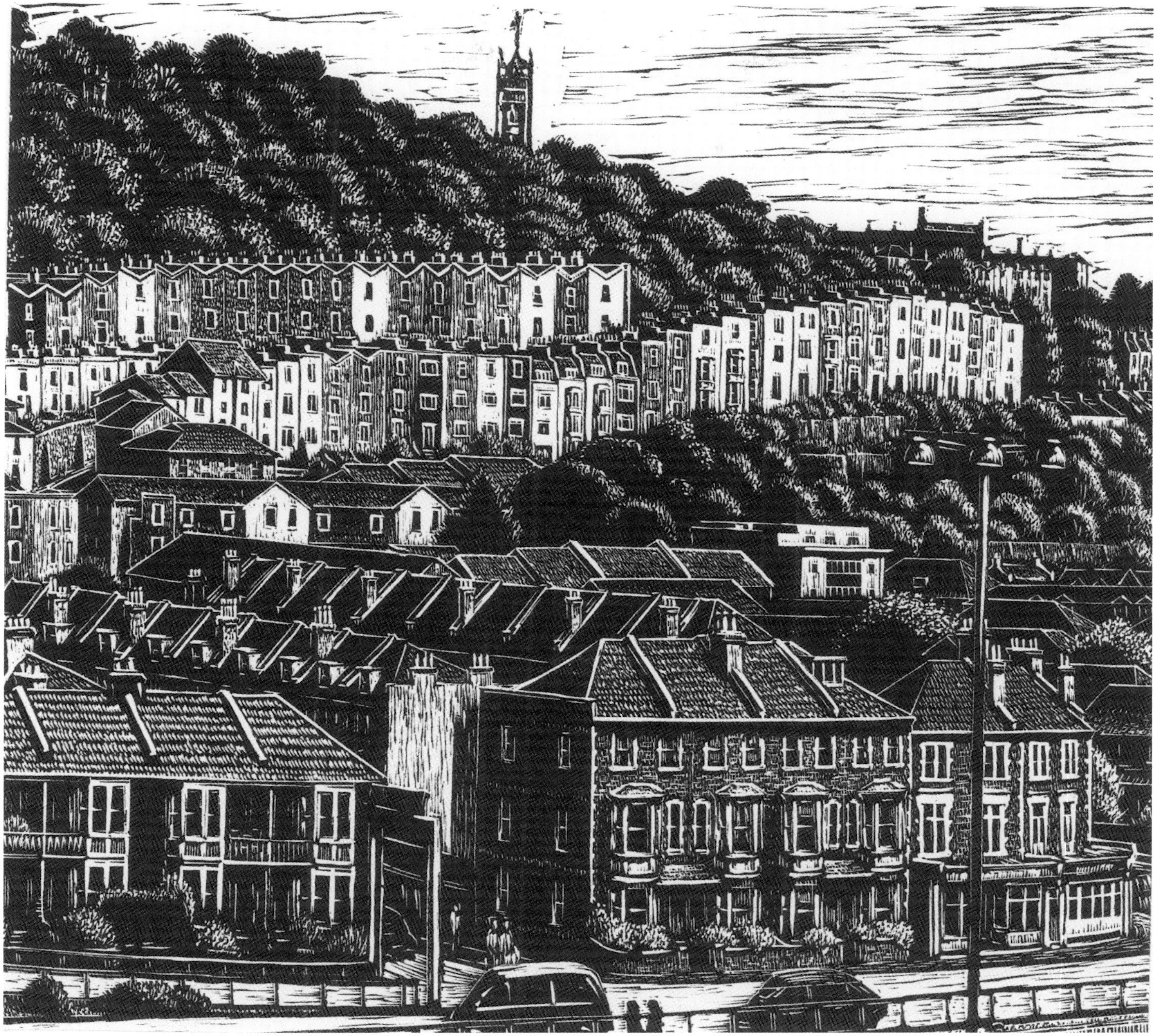

Ambrose Road and Cliftonwood Crescent
with Cabot Tower in the distance.

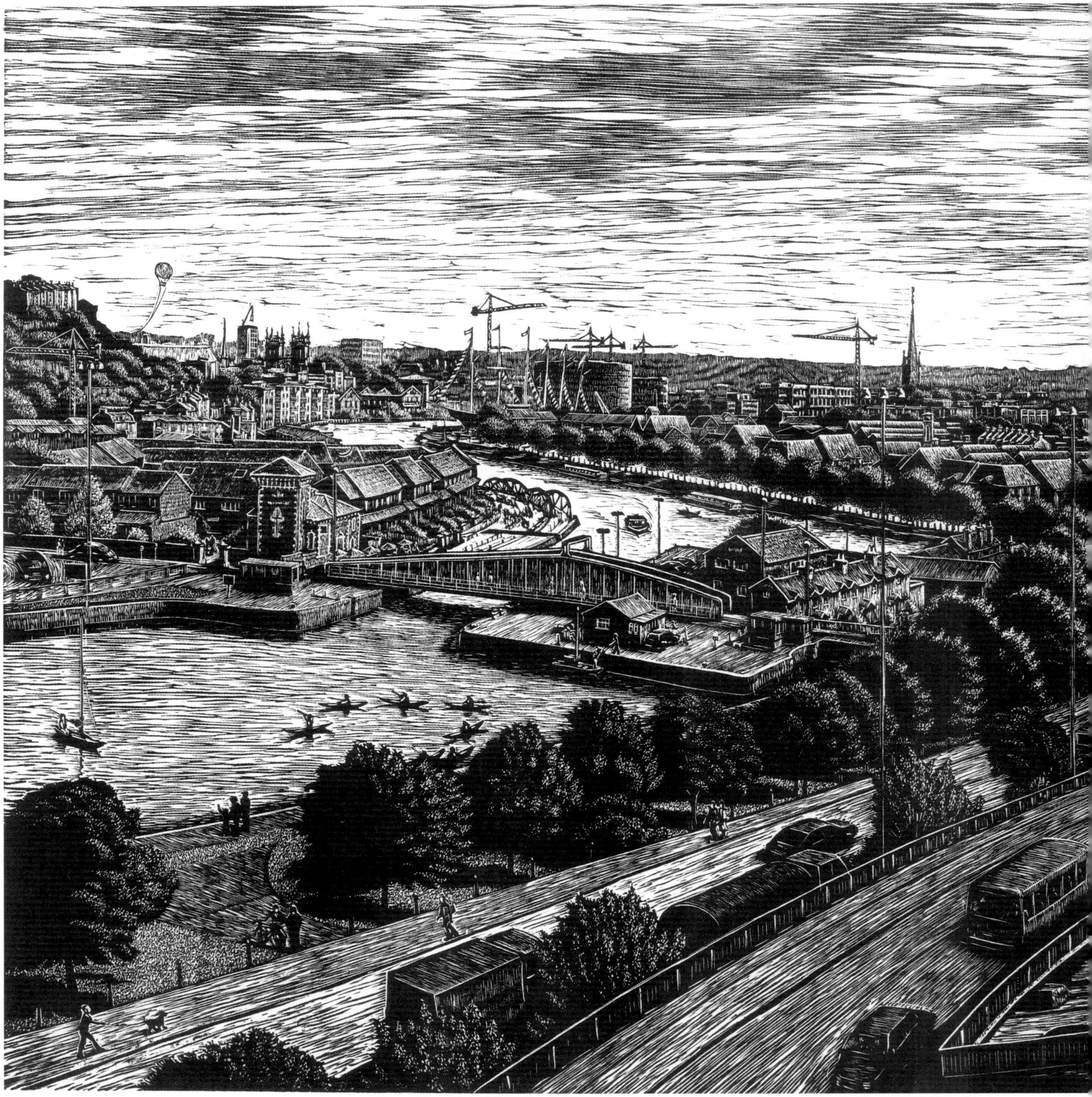

9 *'B' Bond Panorama*
Third block
37 x 79cms (14½ x 31ins)

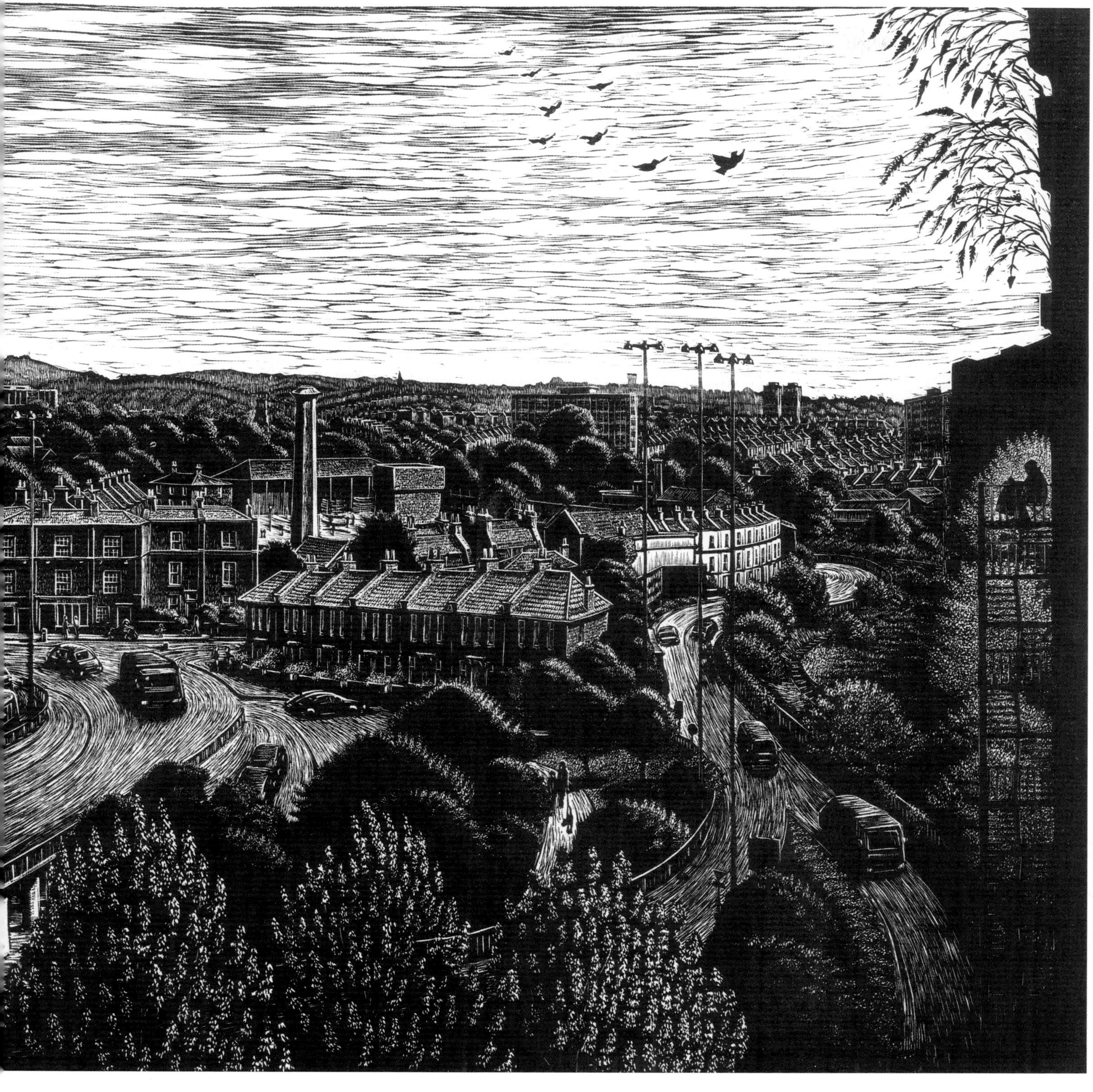

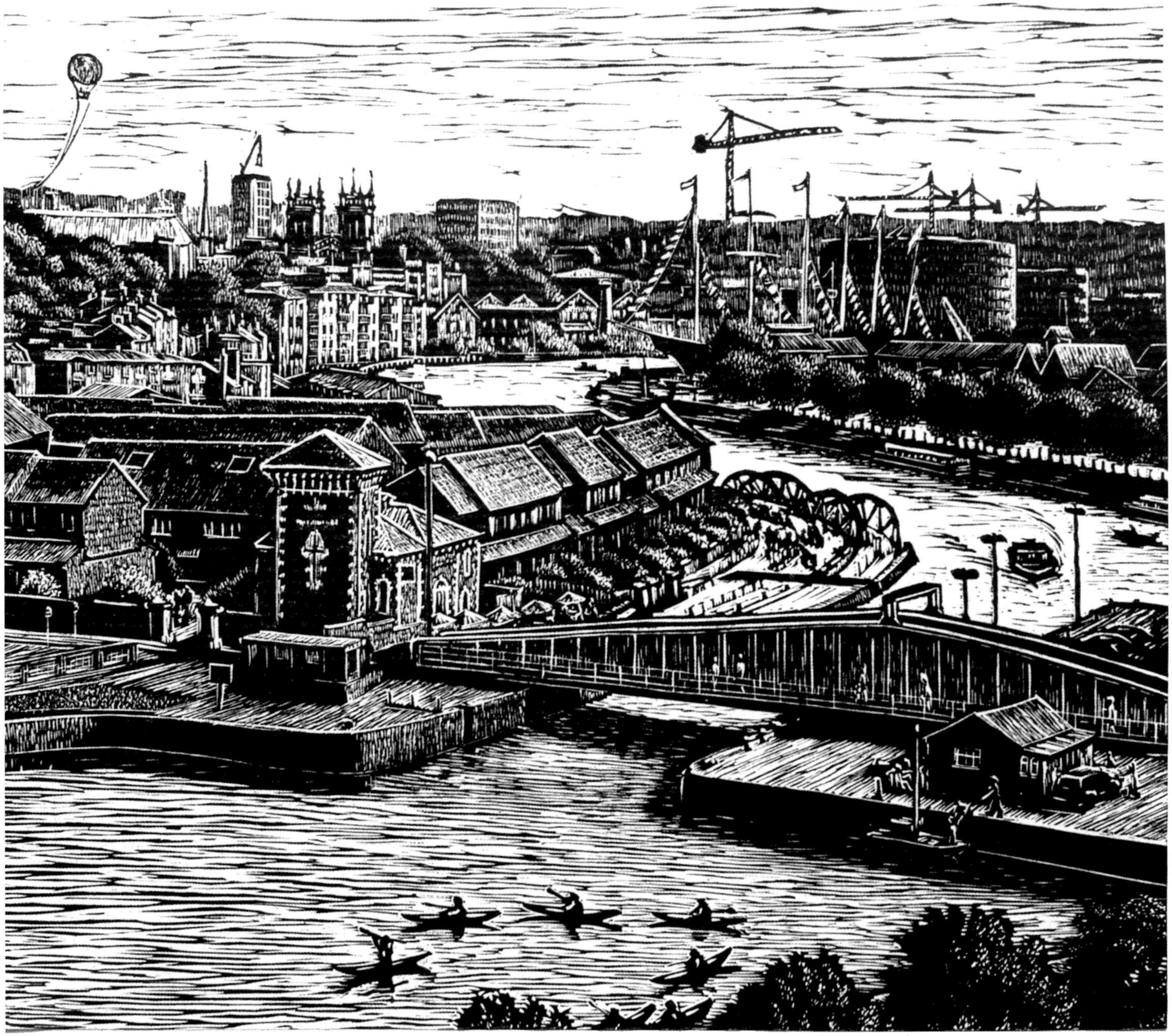

Two actual-size details from the third block.

The Pump House, Baltic Wharf with ss *Great Britain* and Cathedral beyond.

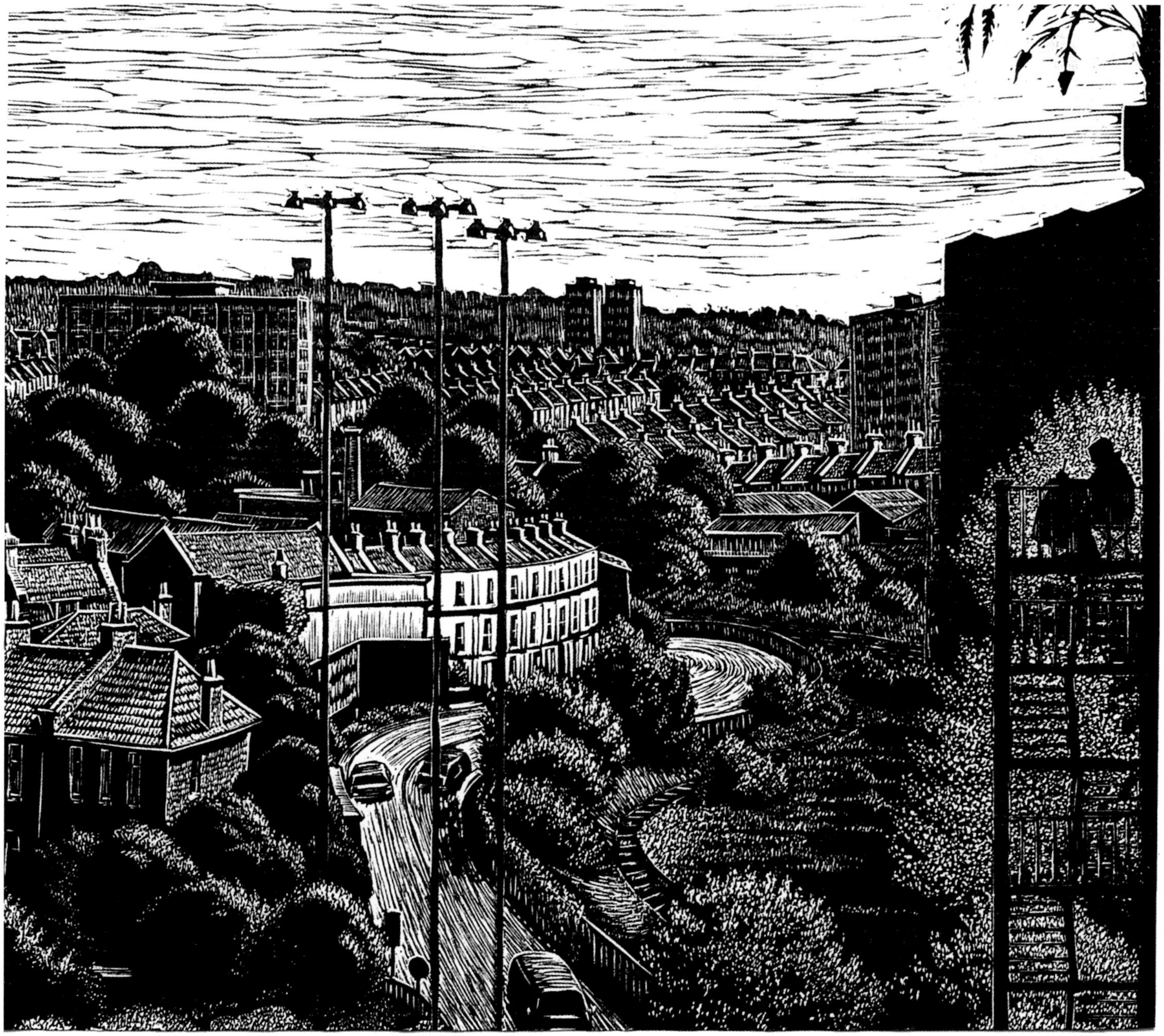

Self-portrait on the fire-escape, making the original sketch, Avon Crescent below.

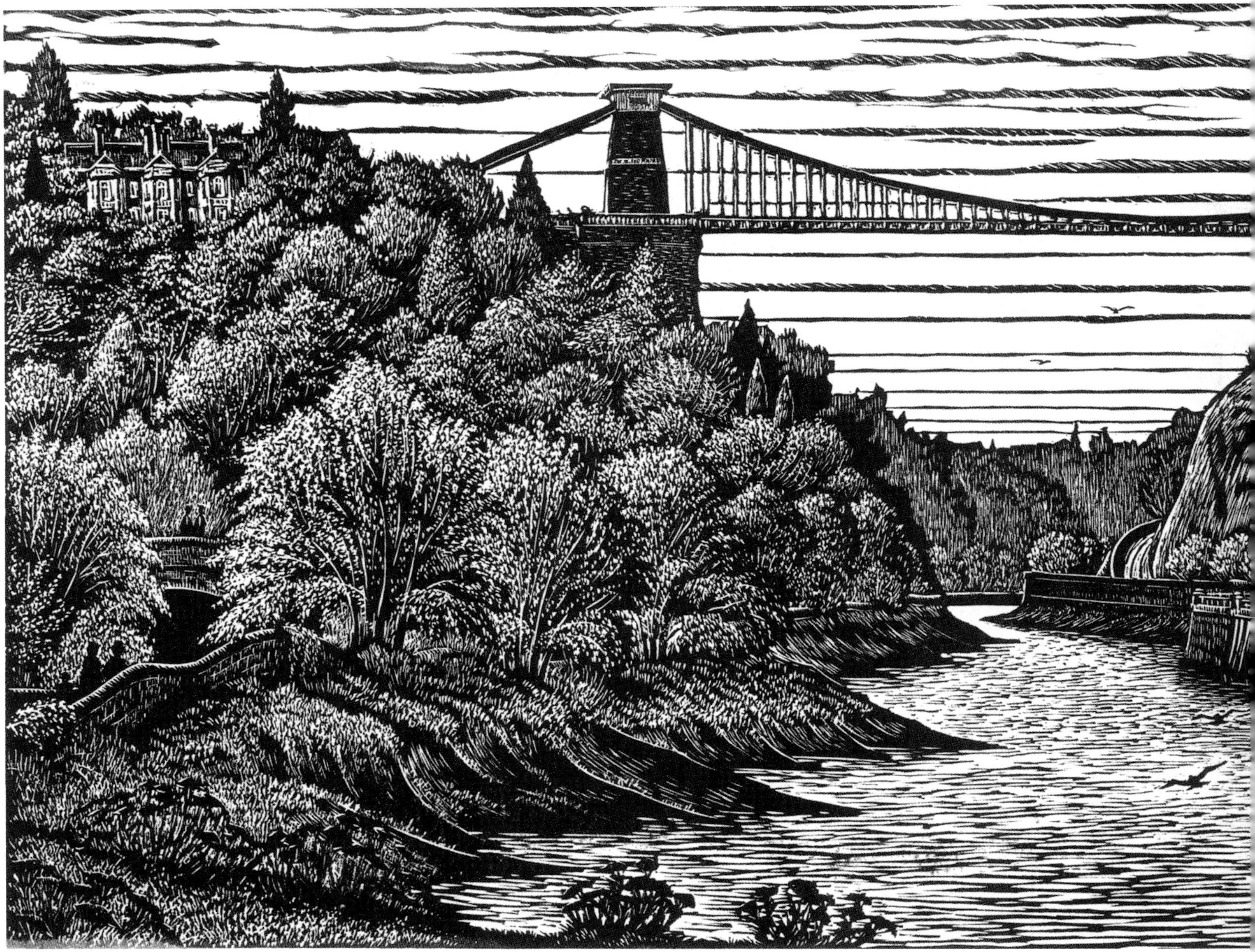

10 *The Clifton Suspension Bridge from Cumberland Basin (spring)*
reduced from 17 x 48cms (7 x 18¾ ins)

I was asked to return to this spot, where I did the sketch for an earlier, much larger engraved version of this subject (Plate 16, 'Panoramic Bristol' 2002) in order to make this smaller version to add to the set of views I have made to these dimensions. I never tire of the view, anyway, as the next two variations illustrated will show.

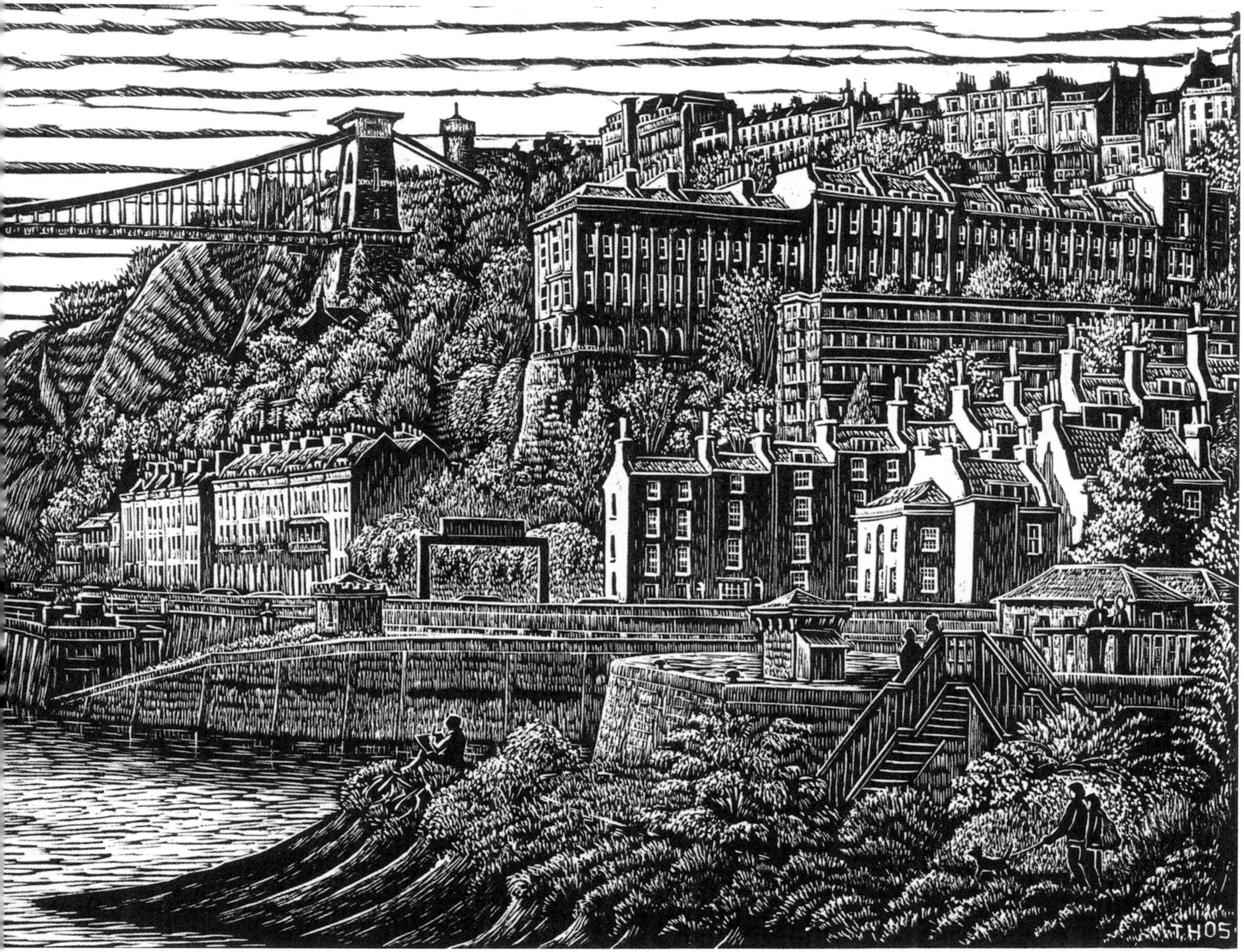
T.HOS

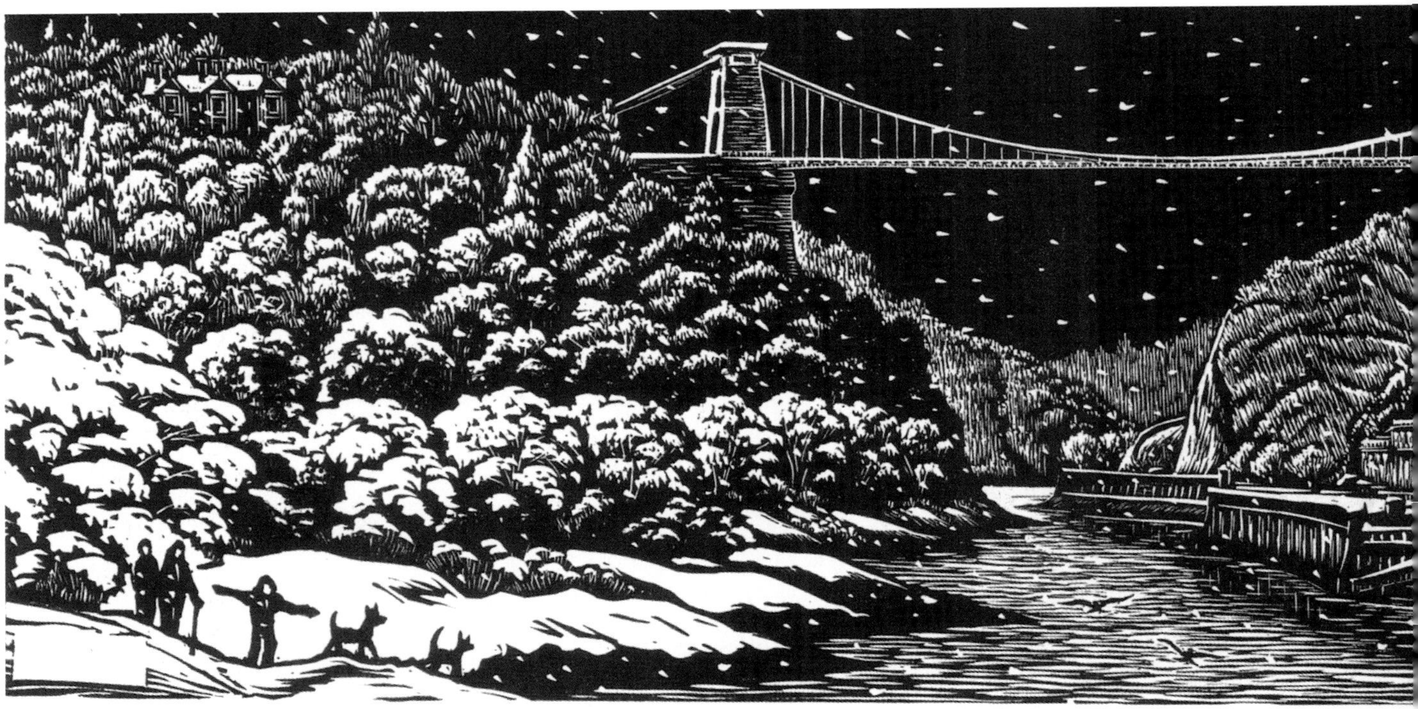

11 *Clifton Suspension Bridge in the snow*
actual size

This version originated as a commission by a design studio who gave copies of some of the original prints to their best clients as Christmas presents. I was keen to do it as I'd already begun a small set of views of Bristol in the snow (which were partly works of imagination as it rarely snows in Bristol these days).

Snow scenes are a gift to any engraver, of course. A light covering simplifies the view and creates an interesting play between pure dark and light shapes.

I have often described the process of engraving as like drawing in white on a black surface. These scenes make this most apparent.

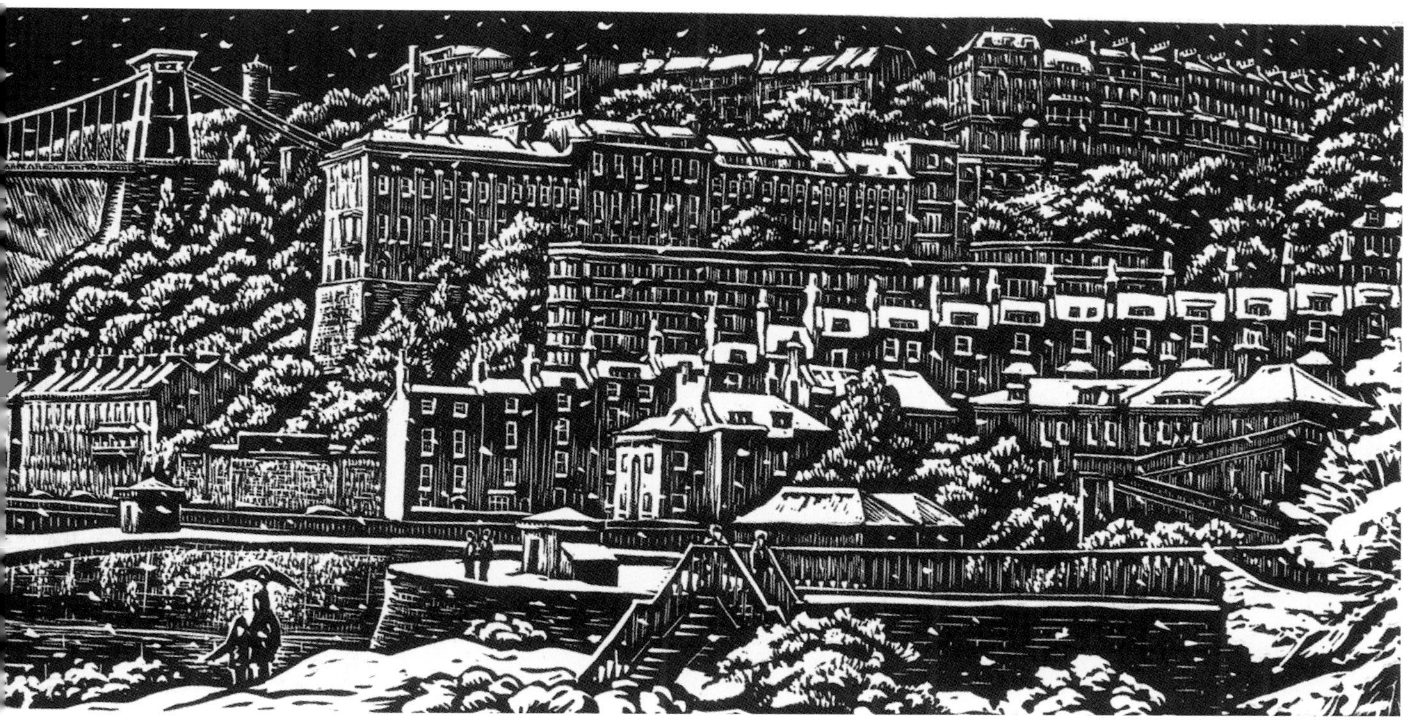

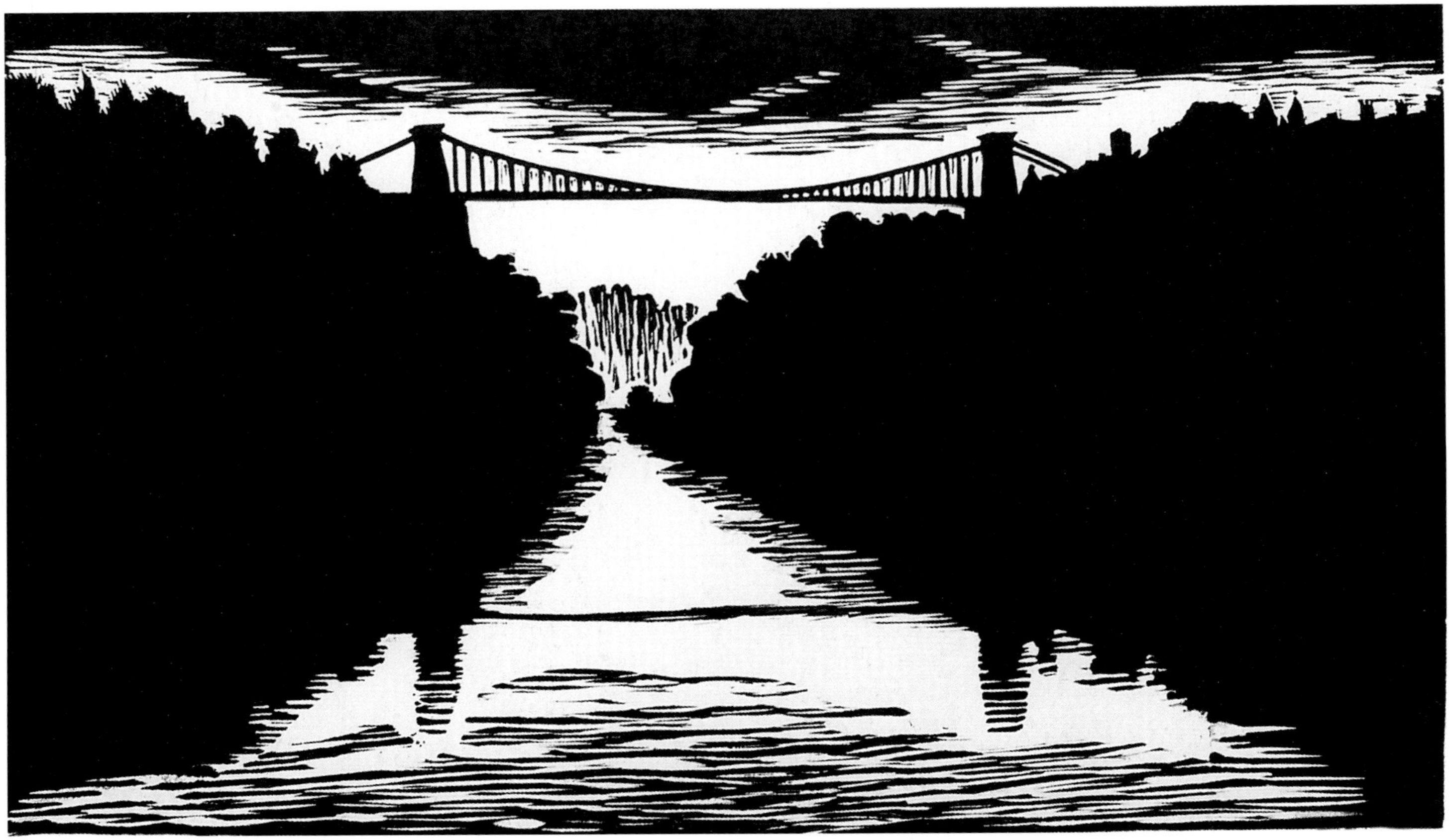

12 *Suspension Bridge silhouette*
actual size

A much simpler treatment emphasising the abstract qualities of the view.

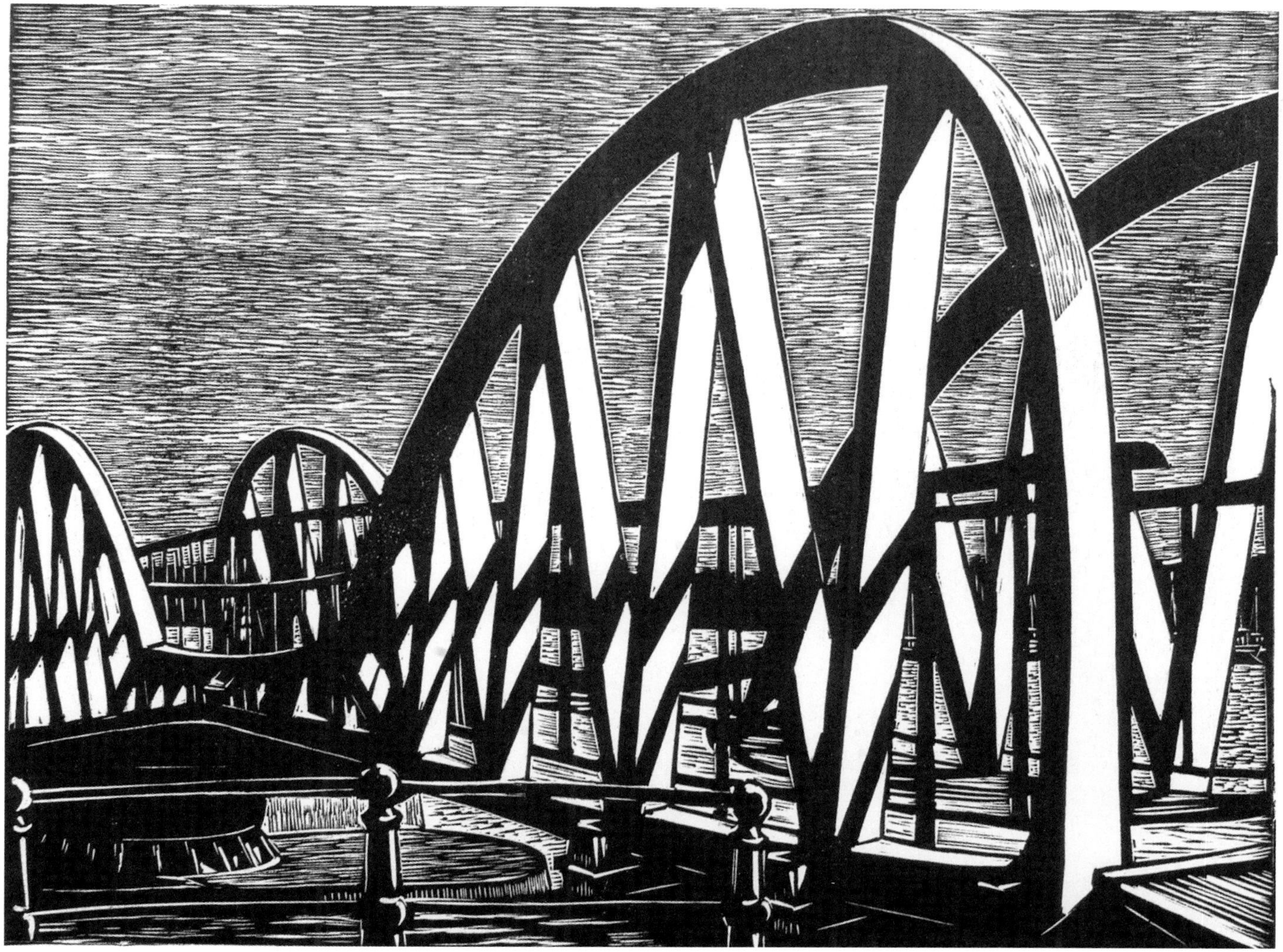

13 *New foot-bridge at Poole's Wharf*
actual size

Walking towards Canon's Marsh, on the dockside, I was attracted by the strong patterns of light and dark on this beautiful example of modern design.

The engraving reminds me of some of the woodcuts of camouflaged battleships by the artist Edward Wadsworth whose work I greatly admire.

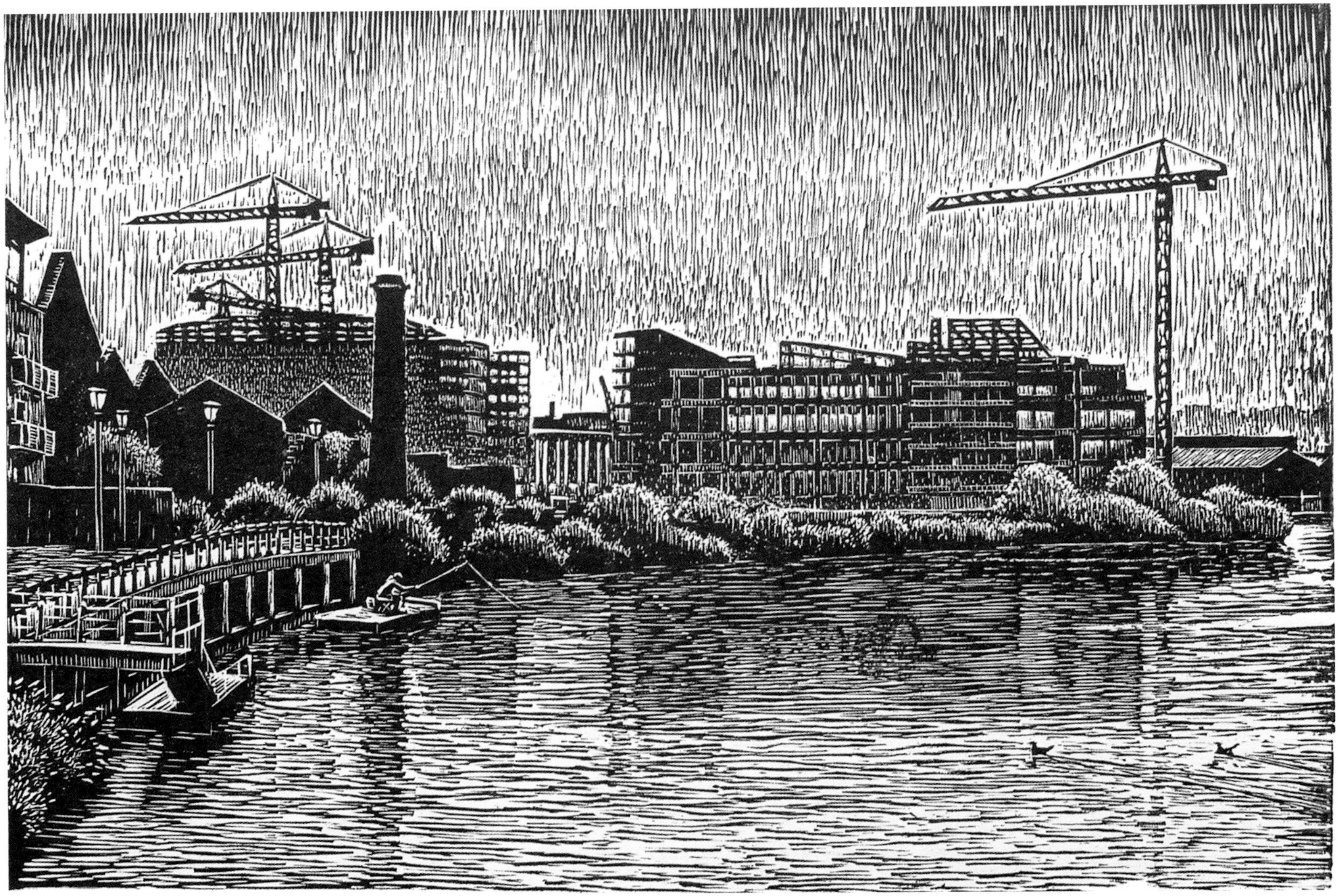

14 *Cranes on Canon's Marsh 2005*
actual size

For this engraving, I returned to the same spot from which I made a study in 2000 (plate 4 'Panoramic Bristol'). This part of the city is in a dramatic state of flux these days and will be so for some time to come.

It is to be hoped that when these buildings are completed they will be architecturally outstanding and fully merit their position on this unique site.

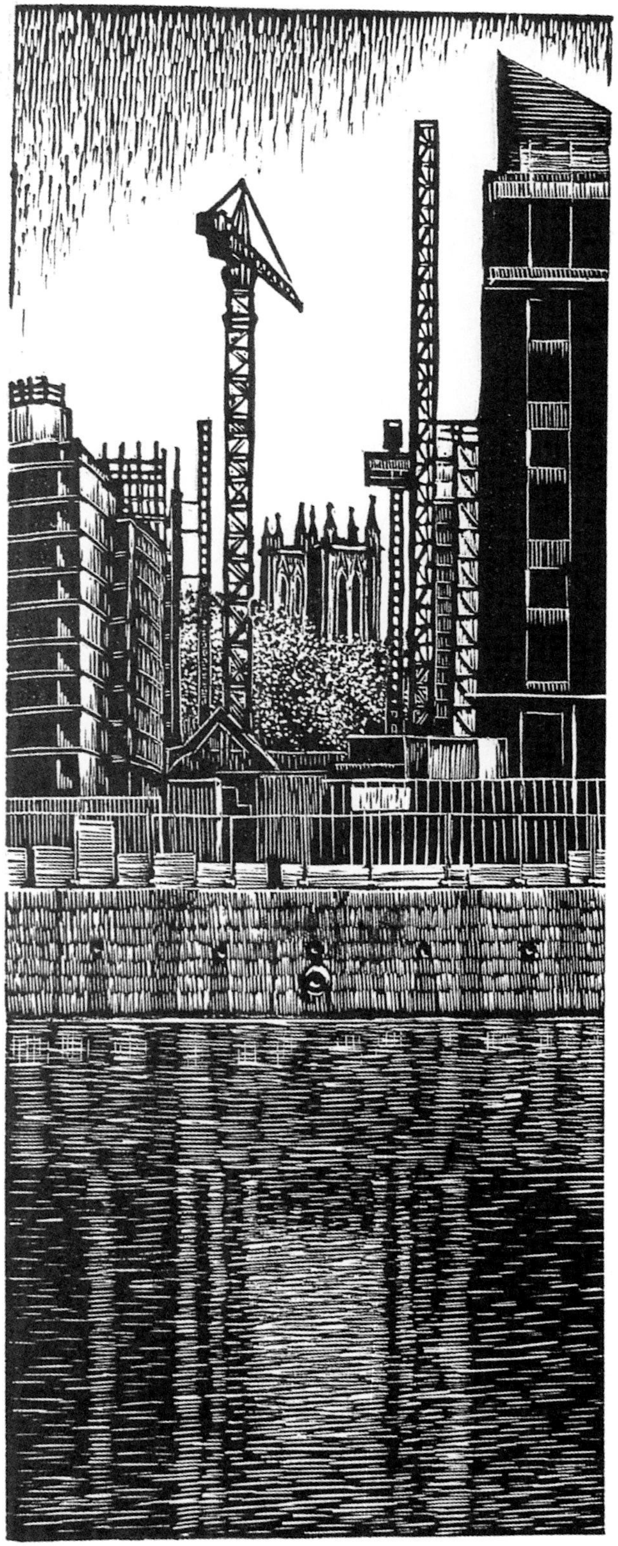

15 *Bristol Cathedral from Prince's Wharf*
actual size

This is the much trumpeted 'preserved view' of the Cathedral between new buildings on Canon's Marsh.
I enjoyed trying to engrave the filigree silhouettes of the cranes and the reflections in the water at this stage of the building work.

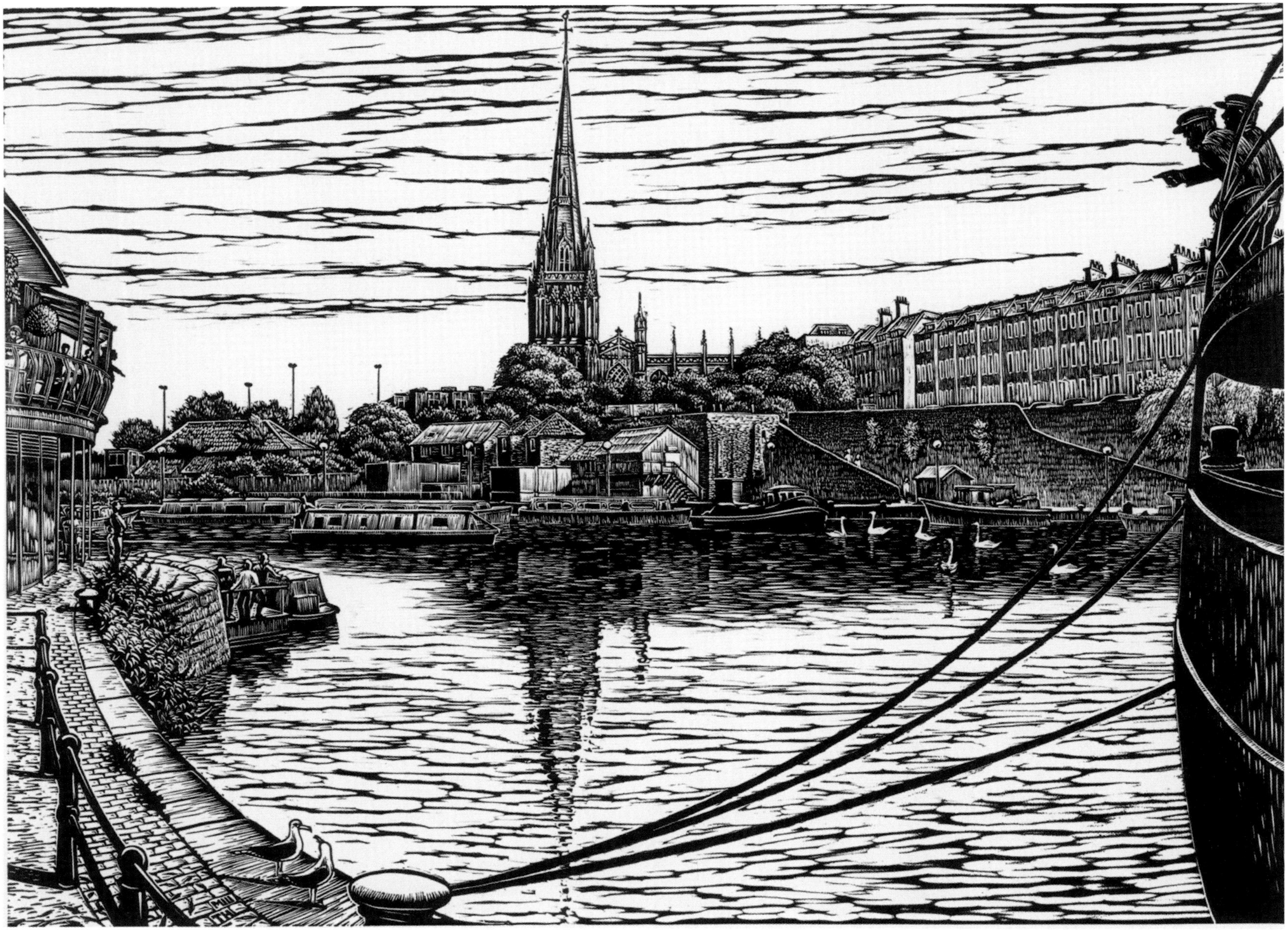

16 *Redcliffe Wharf*

reduced from 29 x 40.5cms ($11\frac{1}{2}$ x 16ins)

This is a return to a favourite spot. This time, I have used the *Thekla* on the right and riverstation restaurant on the left as framing devices to the composition.

This illustration is, in fact, the final key-block of a set of three I made in order to produce coloured versions of the design in the manner of Japanese wood-block prints.

I have enjoyed working in both ways but still like the strength of pure black and white.

Around the City Centre

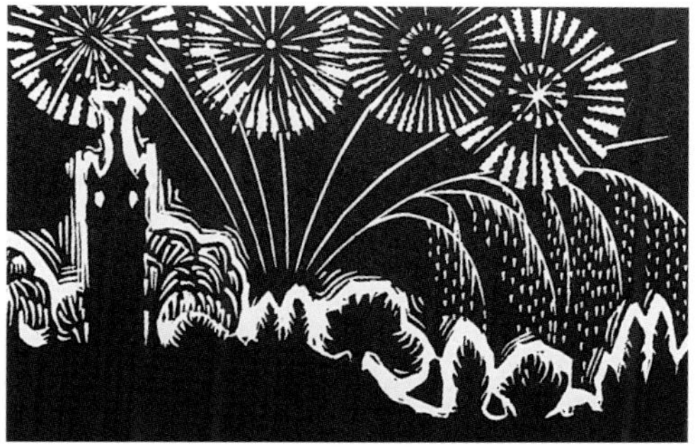

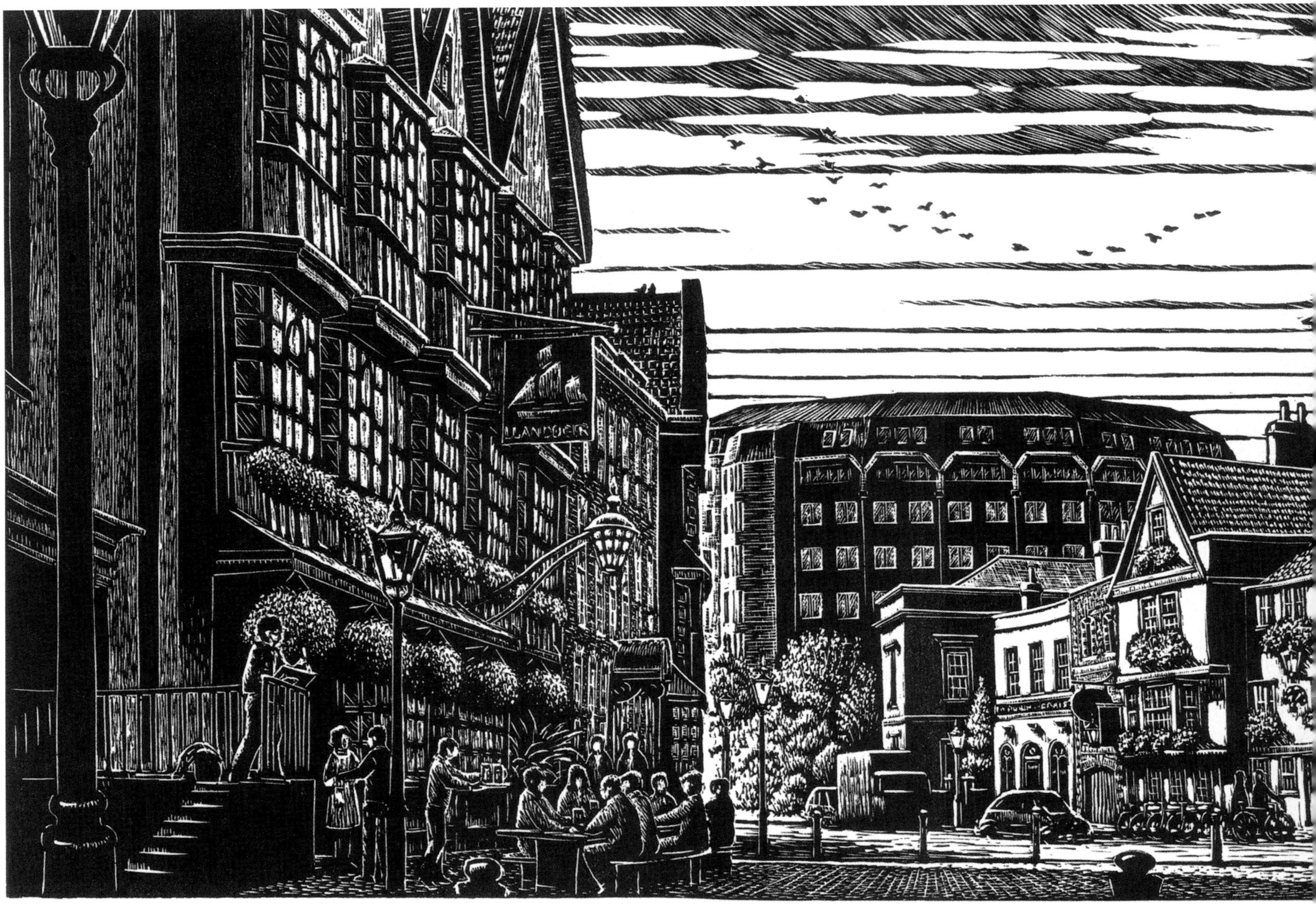

17 *King Street*
reduced from 17 x 48cms (7 x 18¾ ins)

The Llandoger Trow is on the left, the Theatre Royal on the right.
I was shown this street on my very first visit to Bristol almost 40 years ago. It made a lasting impression and I've often drawn and painted there.
This is my first engraving of it and I thought the wide-angle format suited it well. The whole street is like a stage set.

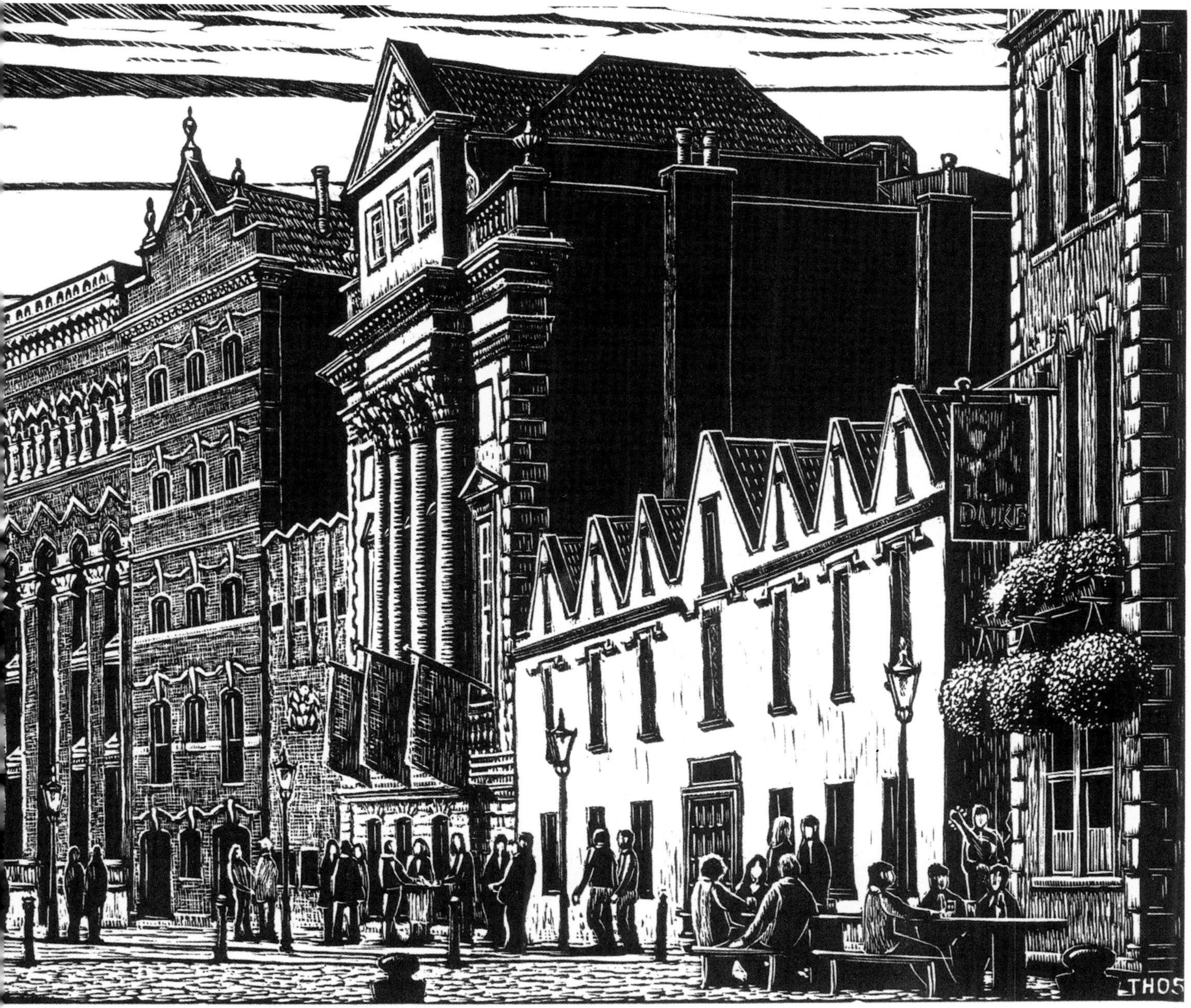
DUKE
THOS

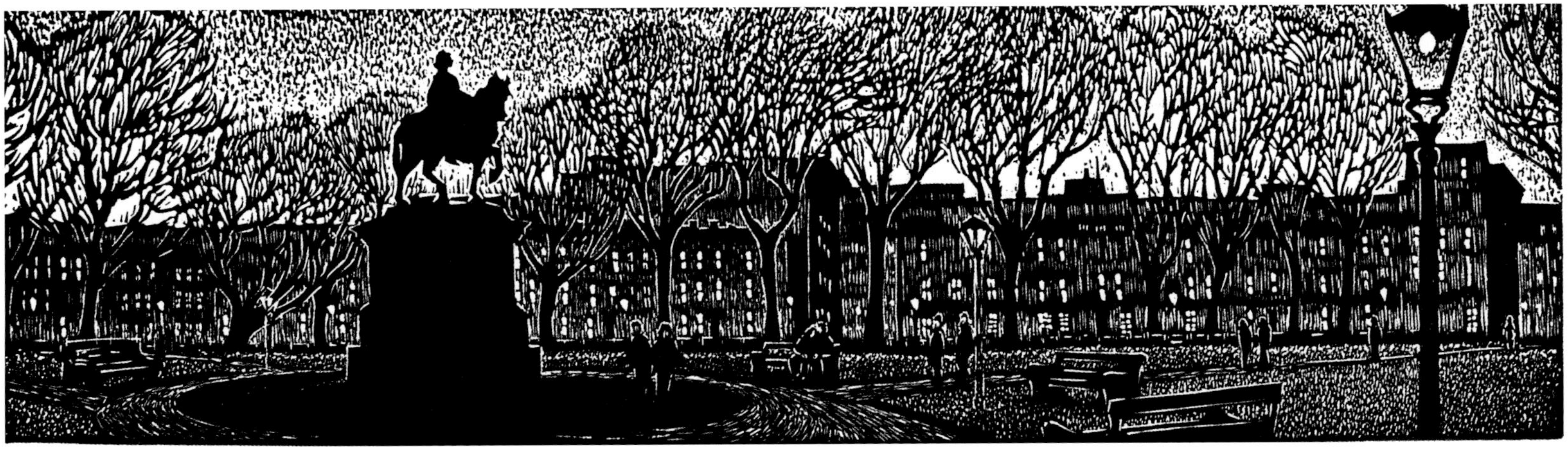

18 *Queen Square: autumn evening*
actual size

The restoration of this Georgian square is a credit to the city. The famous equestrian statue of William III by Rysbrack now forms a proper focal point.
The surrounding plane trees are an attractive feature, too.
In this engraving, I was trying to convey the atmosphere of a November evening.

19 *The Rysbrack statue of William III*
actual size

This is a close-up version playing with overlapping silhouettes.

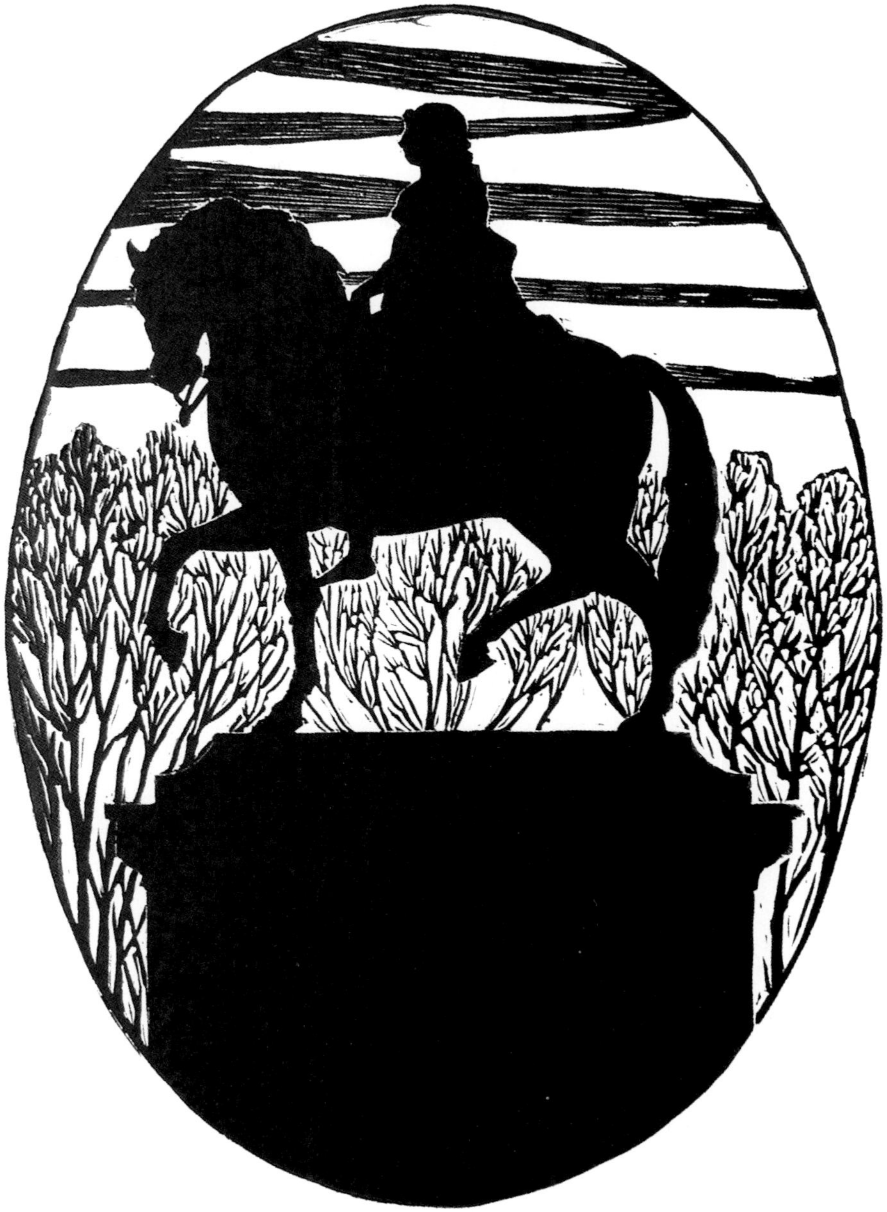

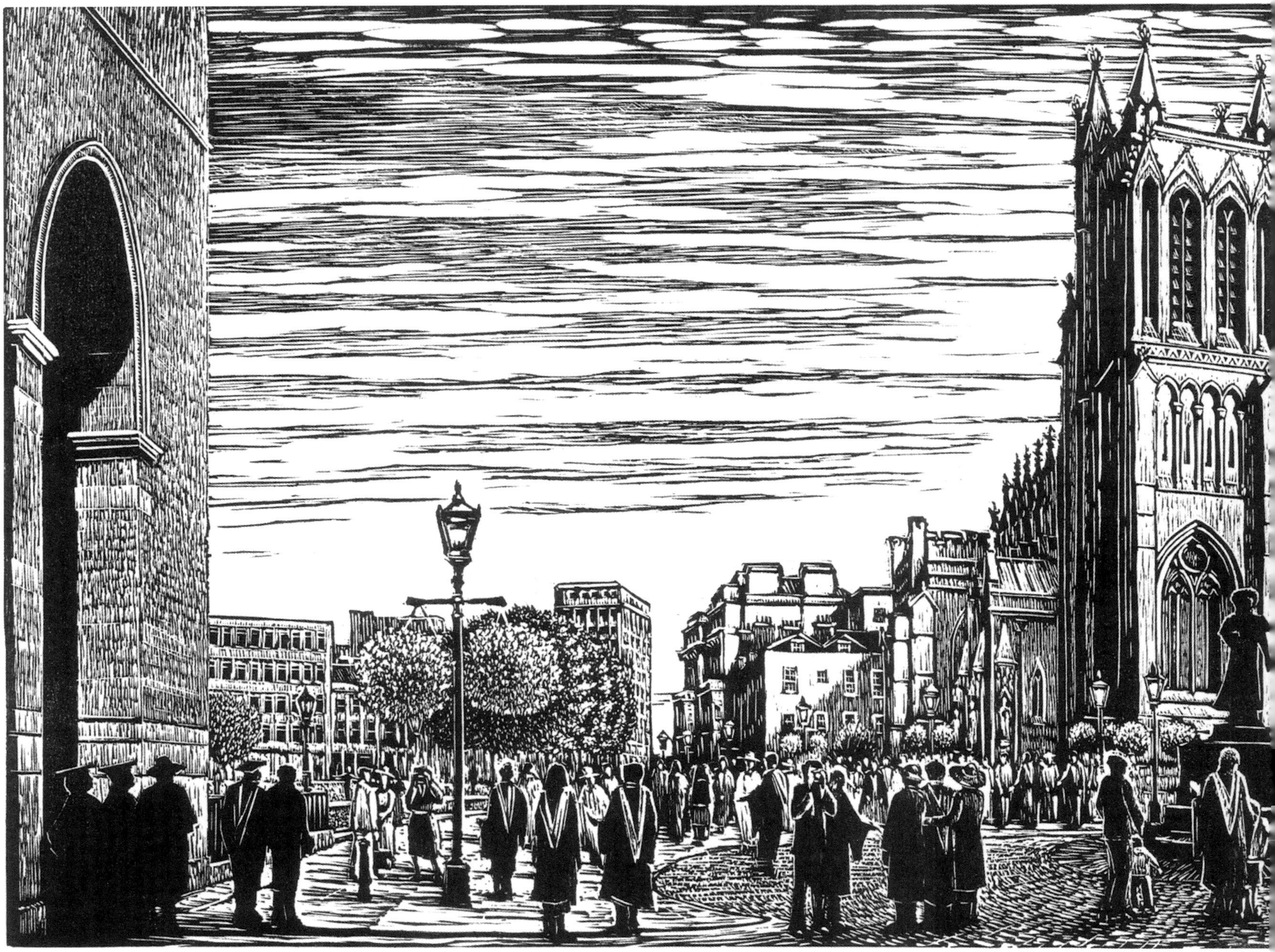

20 *The west end of Bristol Cathedral, with Gatehouse and main entrance of the Central Library (Graduation Day)*
reduced from 17 x 48cms (7x 18¾ ins)

I've been wanting to attempt this view for some time. Seeing it crowded with new graduates in their academic gowns, surrounded by their guests, added extra drama to the variety of architectural forms leading the eye down to College Green.

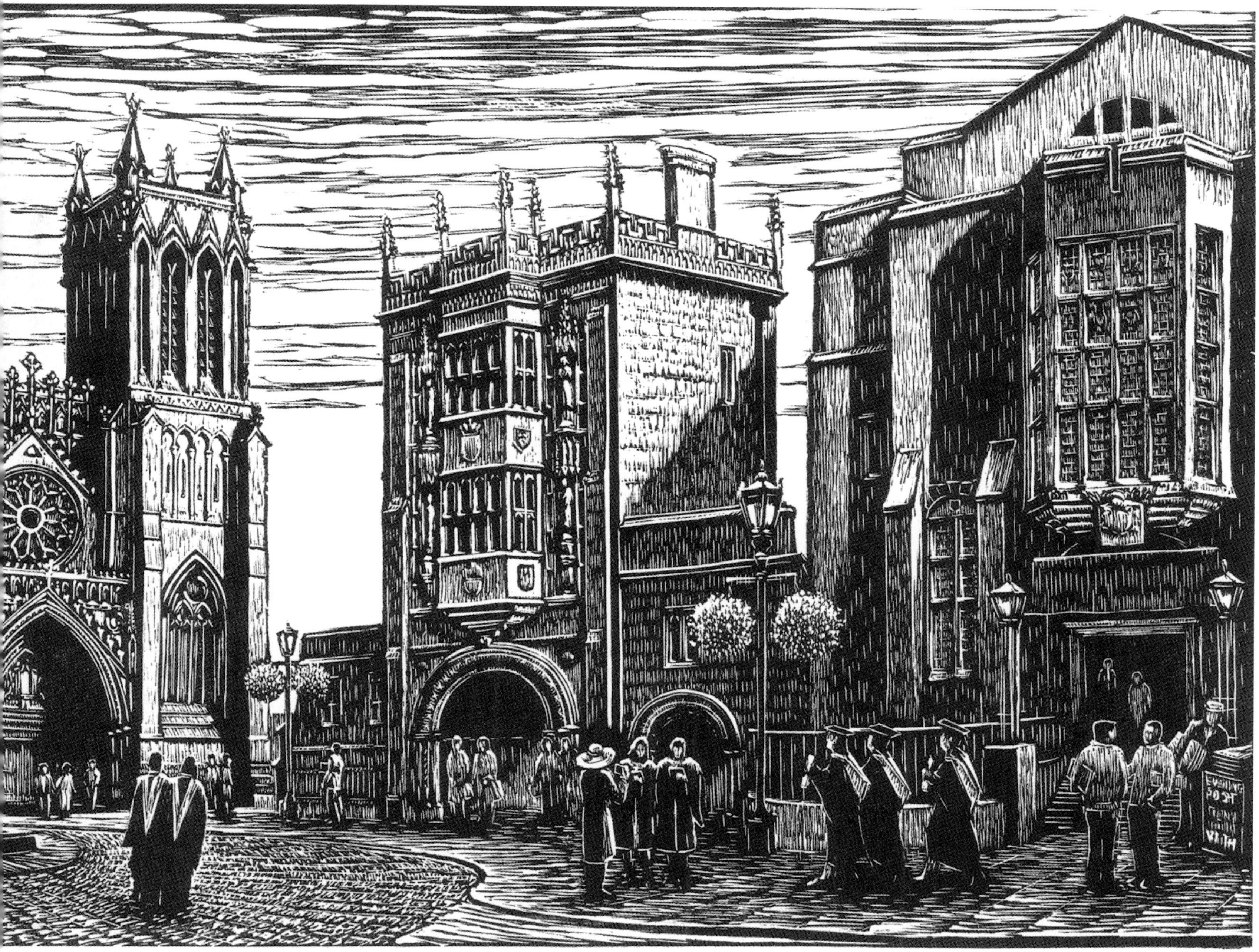
EVENING
POST

Over the next few pages is a group of engravings which form a series of variations on the Wills Memorial Tower at the top of Park Street.

21 *Park Street: afternoon light*
reduced from 48 x 17cms (18¾ x 7ins)

I was able to draw the street from a top-floor apartment in a block nearby but then, with this information in hand, I tried to imagine what it would be like to hover exactly over the street like this.

I particularly like the 'bridge of light' effect which occurs at certain times of the year when the sun shines directly down Charlotte Street (very Wagnerian!). Views which work as a vertical panorama such as this aren't as easy to find as horizontal ones but the hills of Bristol help in this respect.

Opposite is an actual-size detail from this engraving.

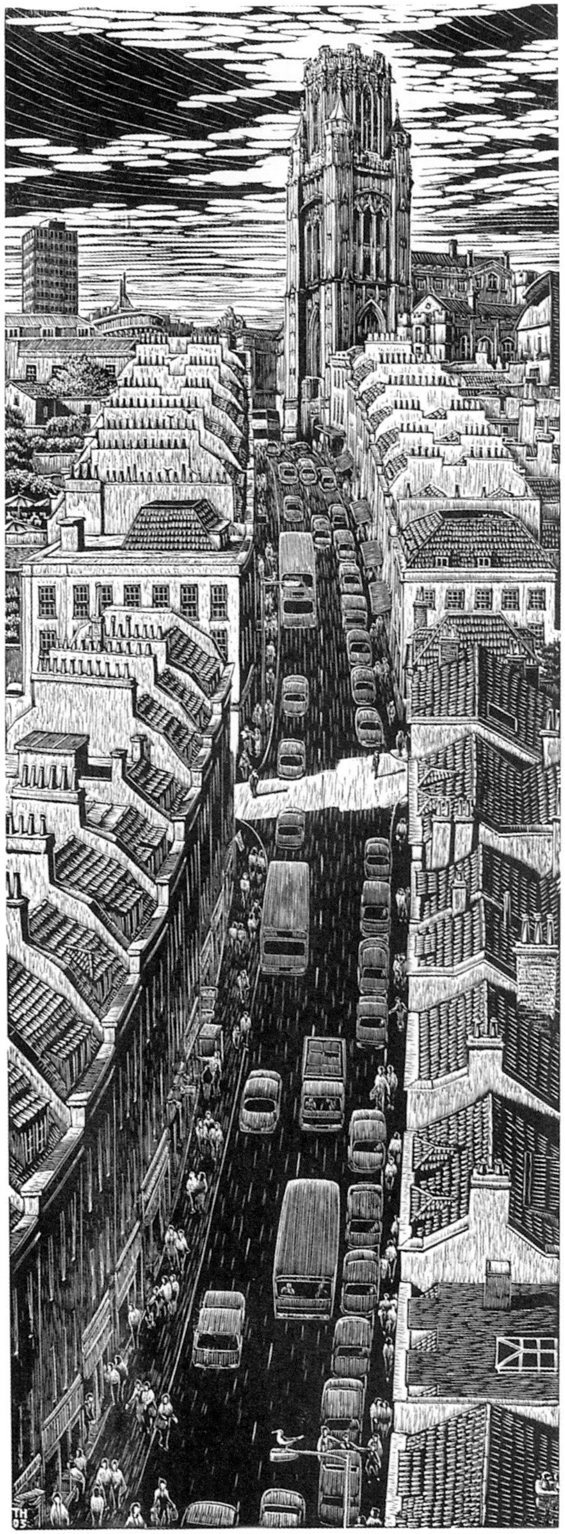

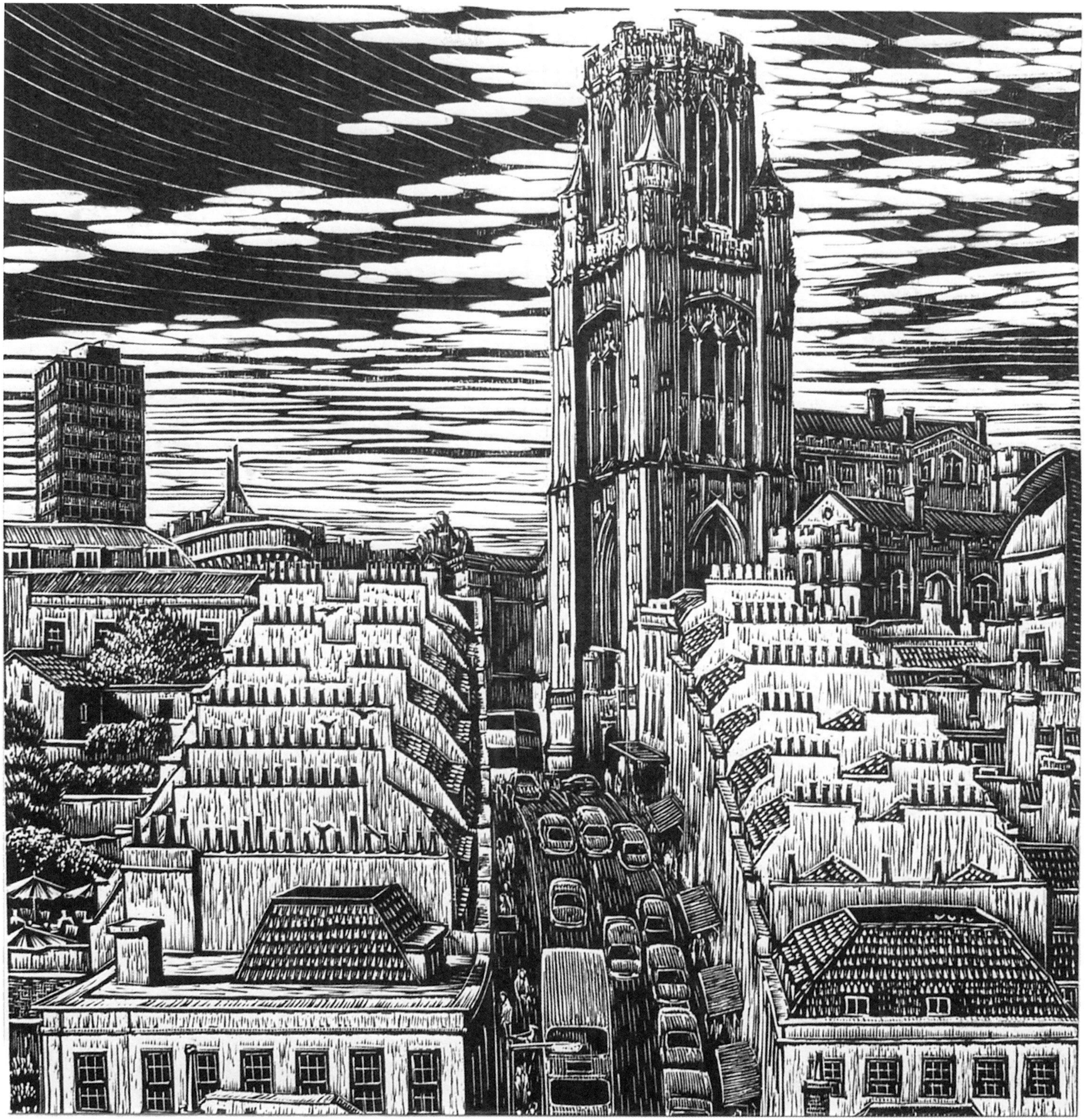

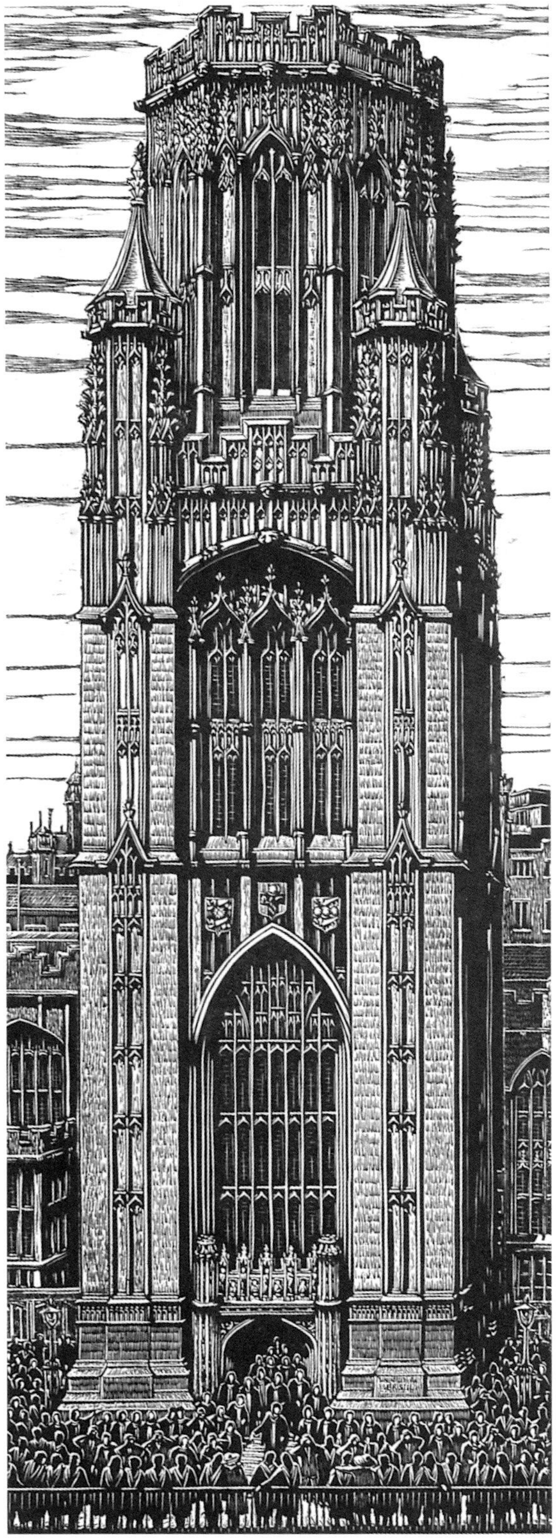

22 *The Wills Memorial Tower: Graduation Day*
reduced from 48 x 17cms (18¾ x 7 ins)

I got to the top of several high buildings opposite to obtain this face-on view of the tower.

From up there, the new graduates spilling out on to the pavements looked like a swarm of black beetles.

The building is such a symbol of Bristol, it is a shock to see old photographs of Park Street without it there.

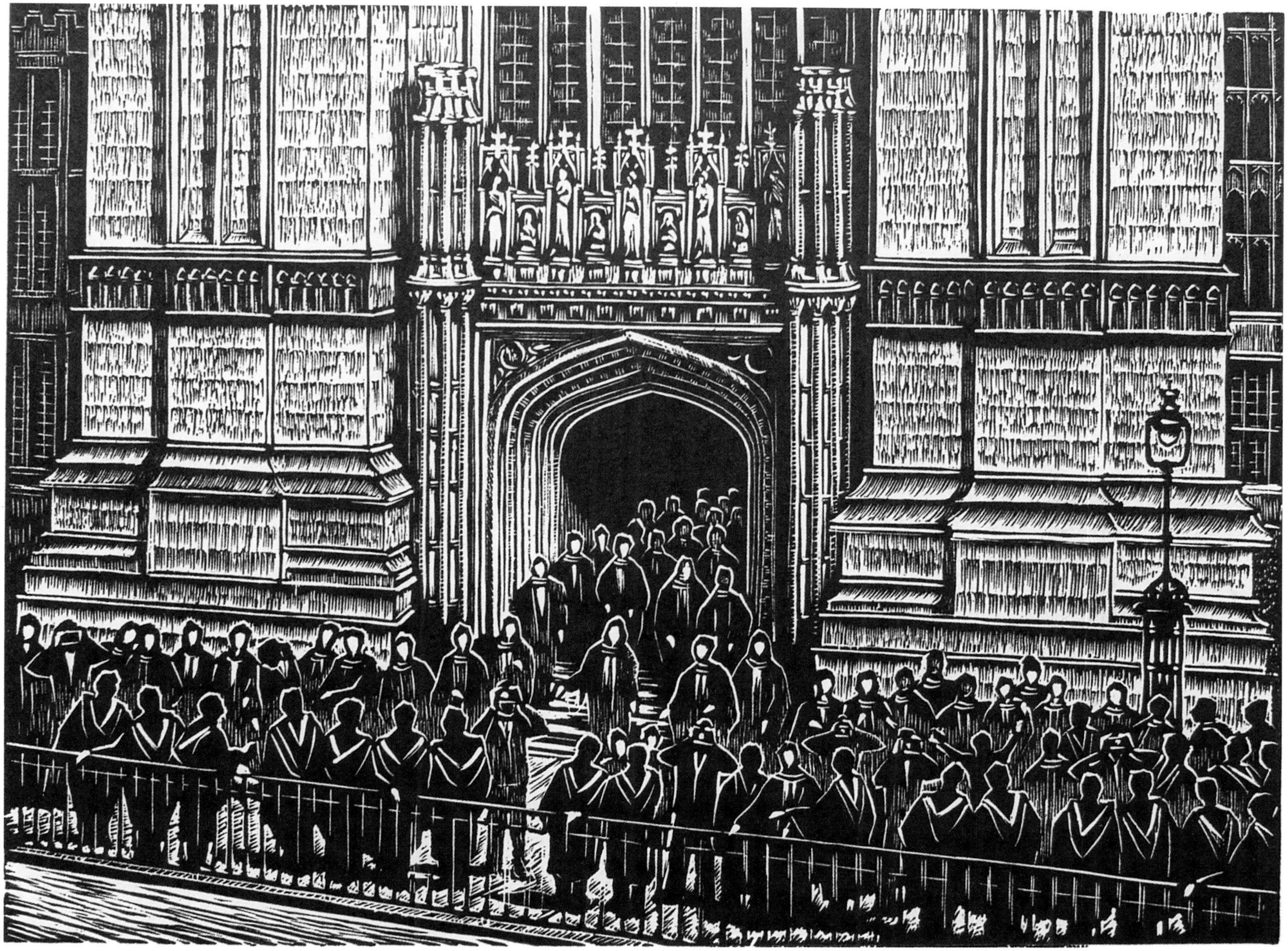

23 *Graduation Day: Main Door, Wills Memorial Tower*
actual size

This is not a detail of the engraving opposite but a separate design altogether. It was, in fact, my first attempt at this subject. I've tried to zoom in and give more prominence to the figures here.

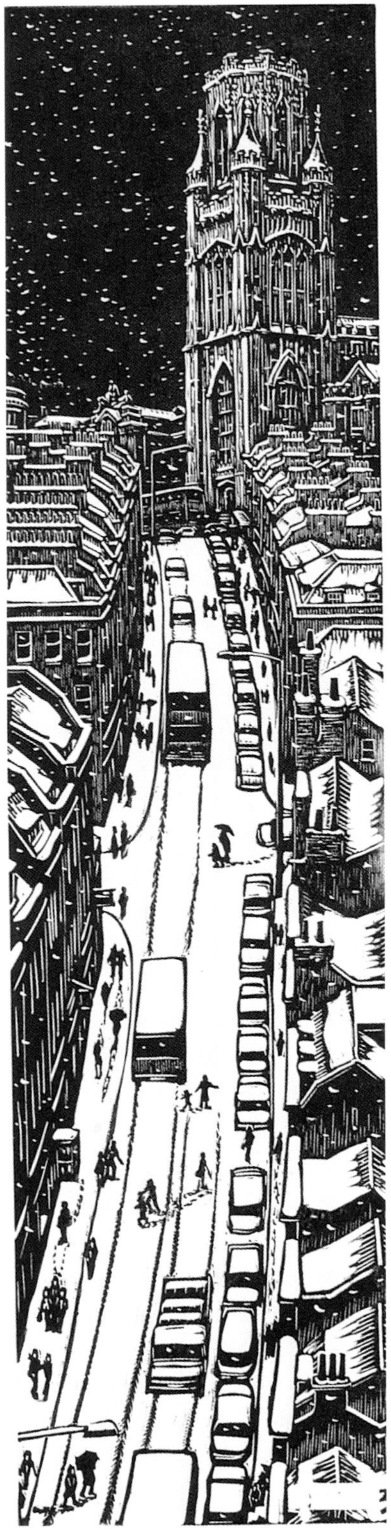

24 *Park Street in the snow*
reduced from 38 x 9cms (15 x 3½ ins)

It is rare to see the street like this but it is a memorable event when it happens. I am always amused by the way the whole area grinds to a halt within minutes of the lightest snowfall.

I went out specially to observe this scene (from ground level) on the one afternoon it did snow in 2003.

I then returned home and produced this re-interpretation of my earlier study.

25 *The Wills Memorial Tower during restoration 2006*
actual size

I turned a corner and found this fabulous pagoda-like structure had suddenly appeared at the top of Park Street in early 2006.

I was beginning to feel I'd produced enough variations on this subject, but this transformation just had to be recorded.

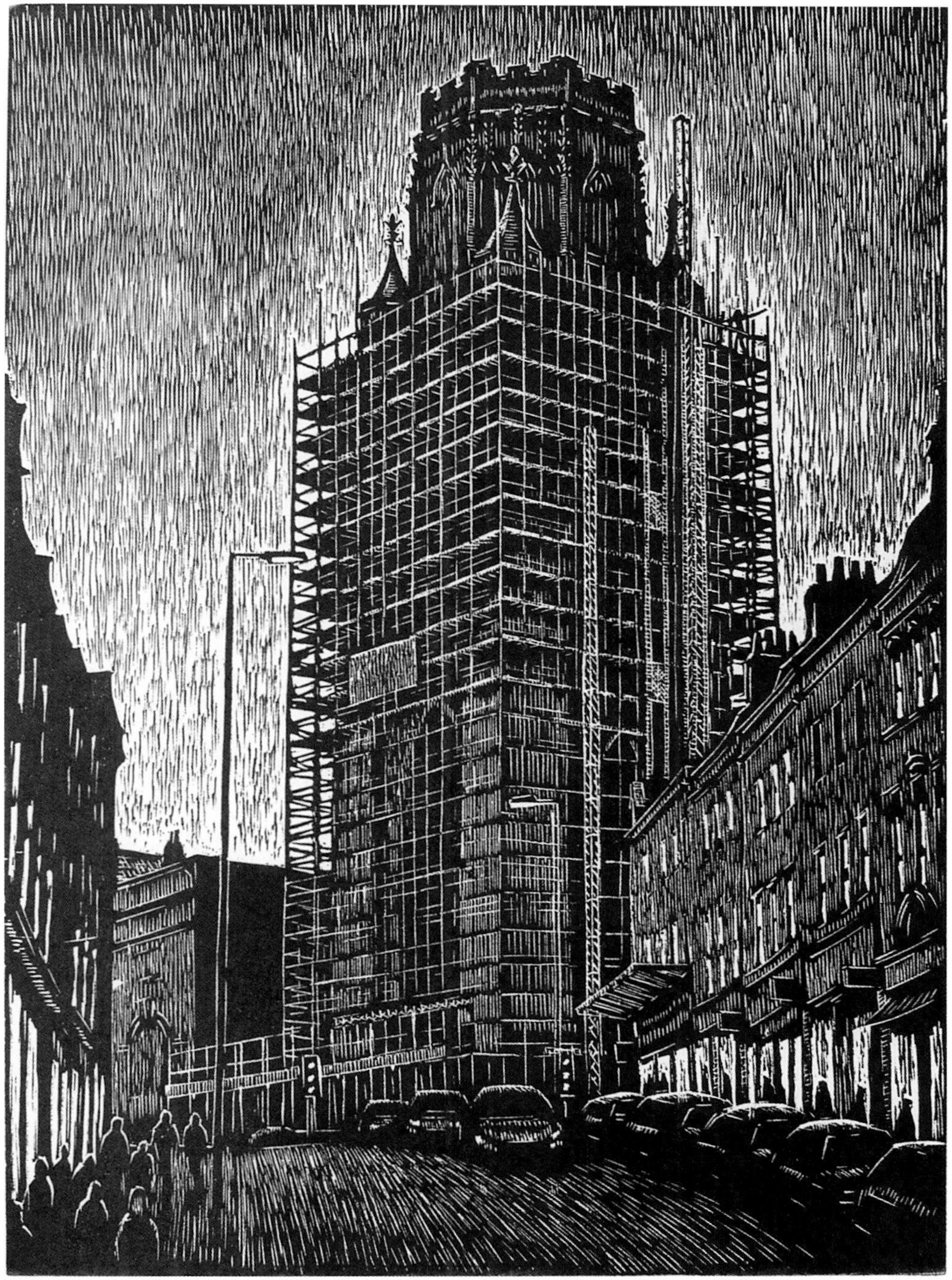

There now follows a series of variations on that other well known Bristol landmark: Cabot Tower on Brandon Hill.

26 Right: ***Cabot Tower on Brandon Hill***
actual size

This was seen from a house in Hill View where I lived for a while in 1999. It was drawn on a windy spring day. I enjoyed trying to capture the sinuous rhythms of the trees and play them off against the more rigid verticals and horizontals of the buildings.

27 Far right: ***Cabot Tower in the snow***
reduced from 38 x 9cms (15 x 3½ ins)

This view is taken from near the top of Constitution Hill, one of the steepest hills in Bristol.

This was the third snow scene I produced of these dimensions in 2003.

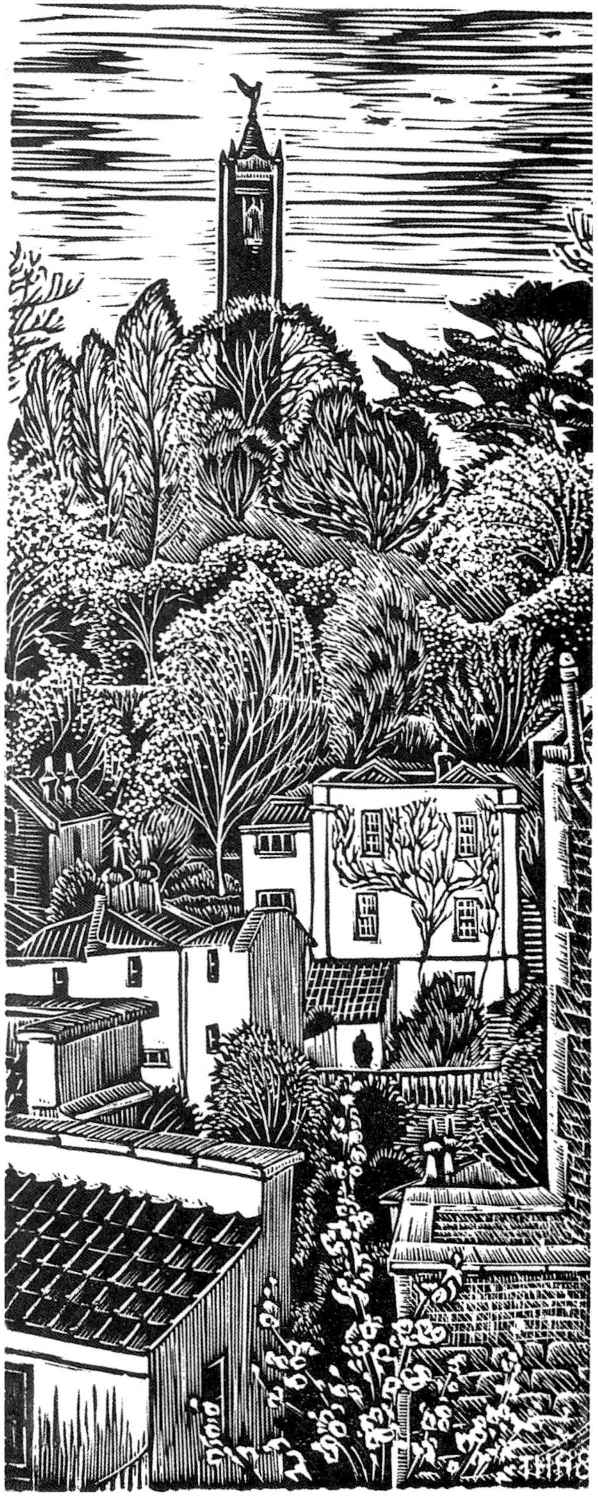

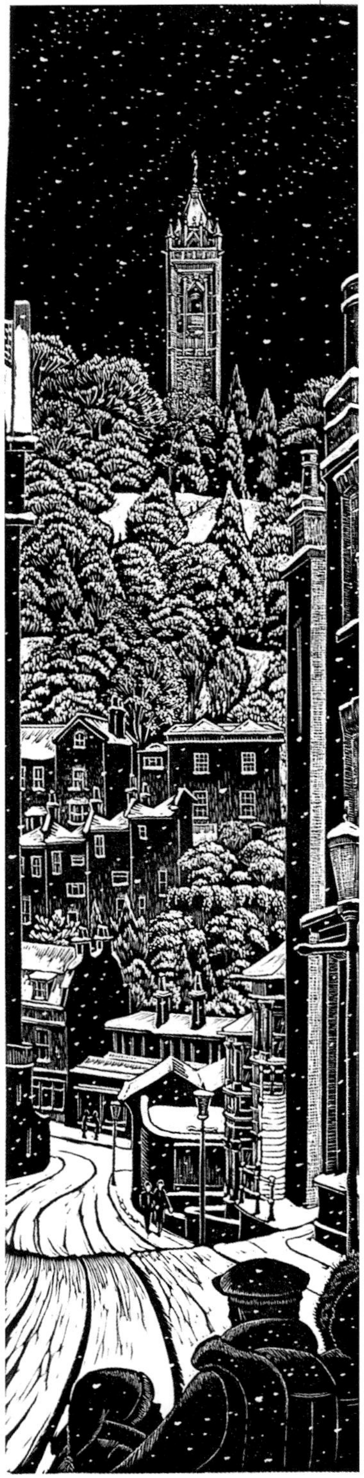

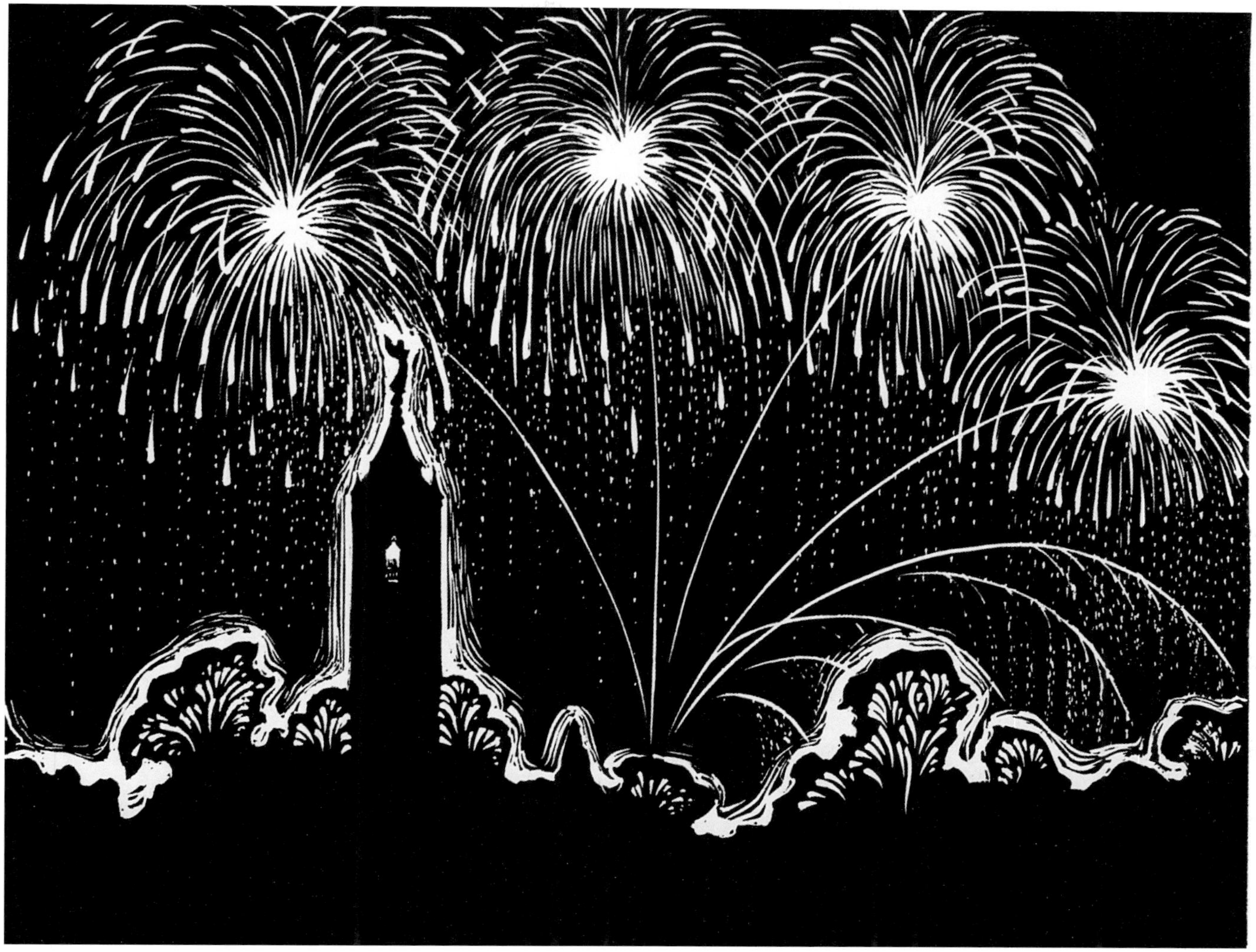

28 *Fireworks on Brandon Hill*
actual size

I often used fireworks as a first engraving exercise for my pupils when I was teaching. The subject allows me to play with creative mark-making with the different tools.

The artist Eric Ravilious also loved fireworks and made wonderful prints and watercolours of them.

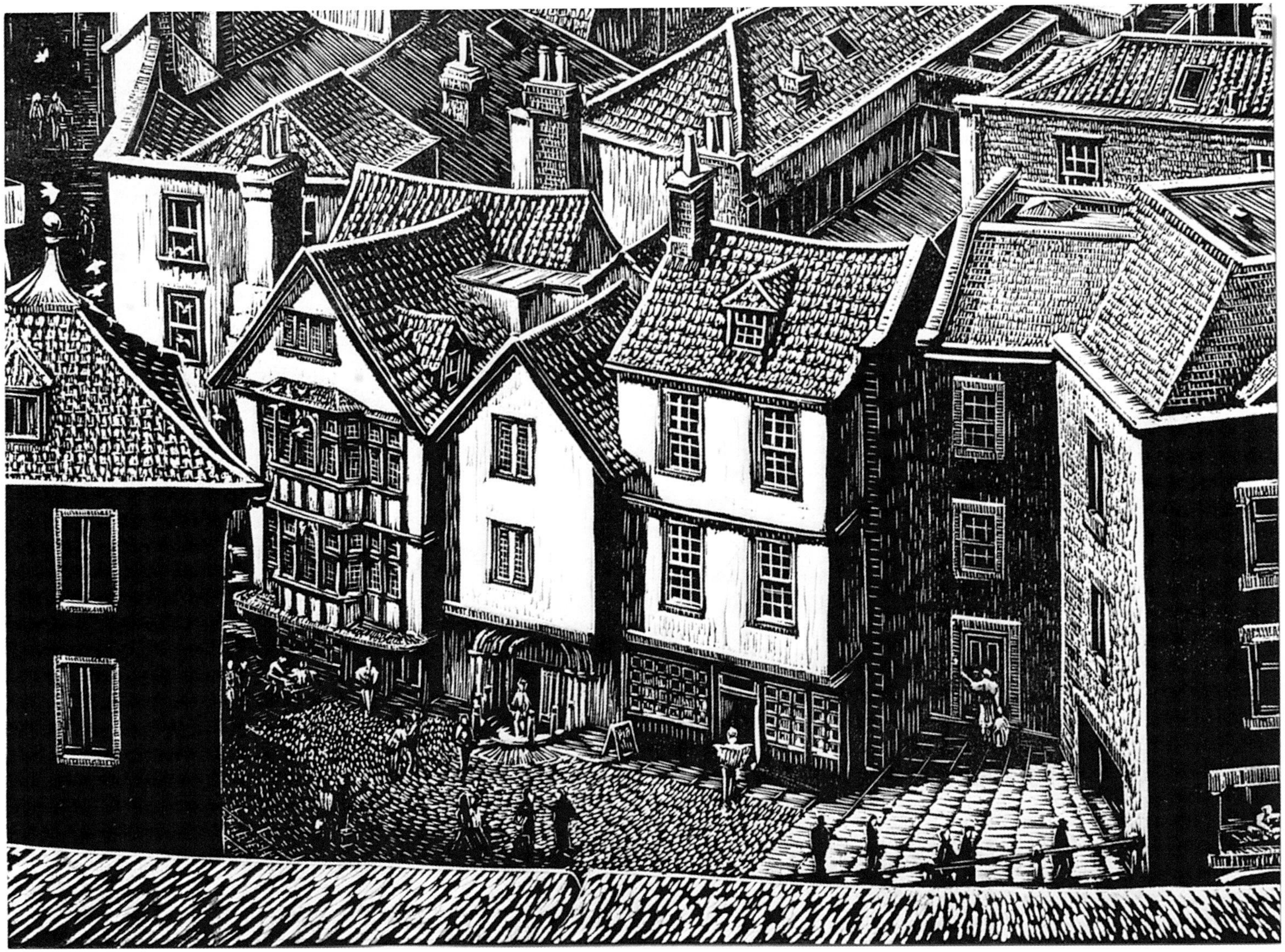

Above: **actual size detail from the engraving opposite**

29 *Christmas Steps, Park Row and St Michael's Hill*
reduced from 37 x 37 (14 x 14ins)

This is my most recent foray into this area – a view directly down onto the steps and the first composition where I have been able to include both the steps and St Michael's Hill. I found it an almost mesmerising exercise to engrave it.

At the top of the steps, on the far side of Colston Street, can be seen the balcony of the new bar/restaurant, Zero Degrees. The sketch for plate 30 illustrated on pages 62 and 63 was made from there.

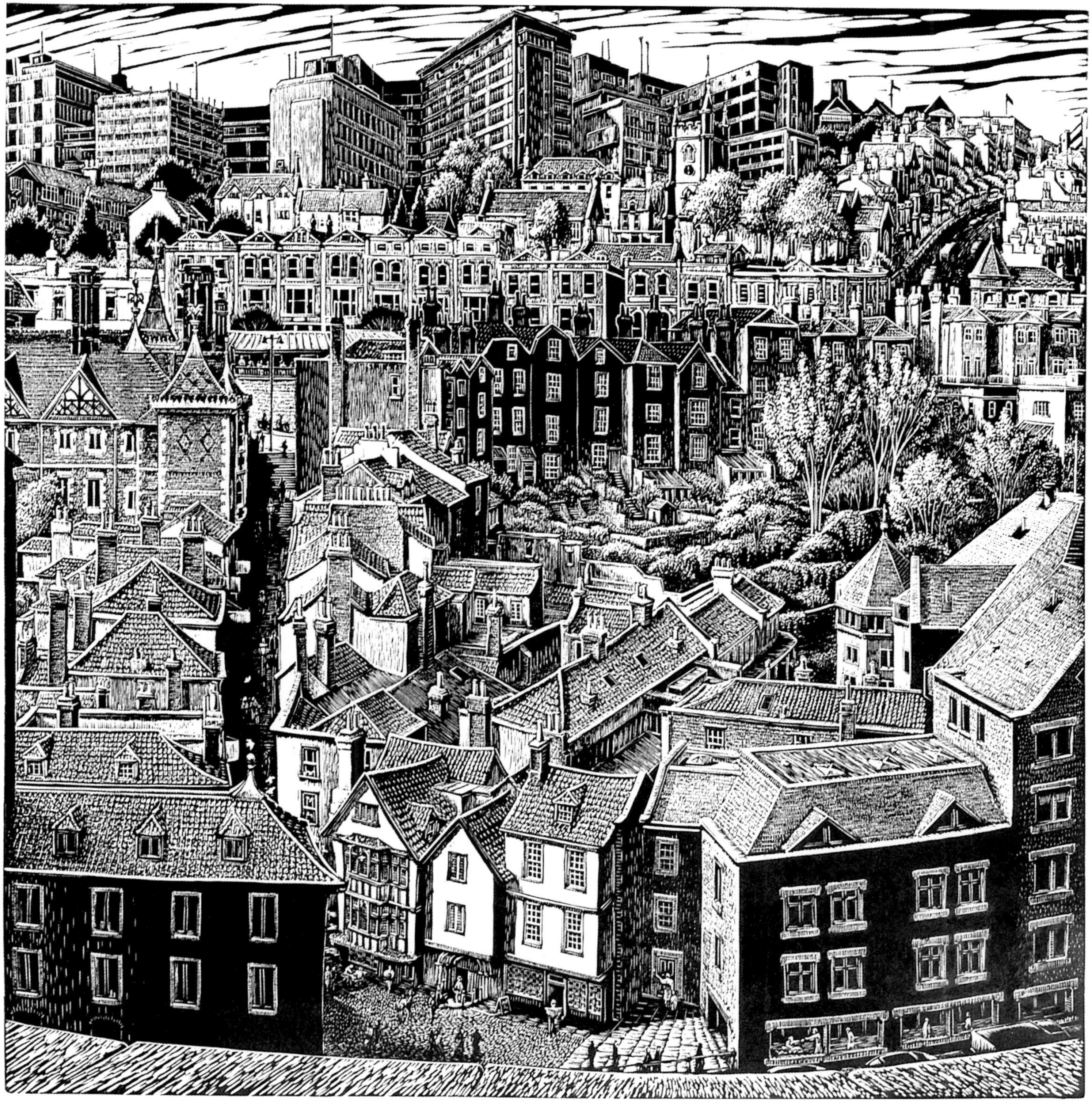

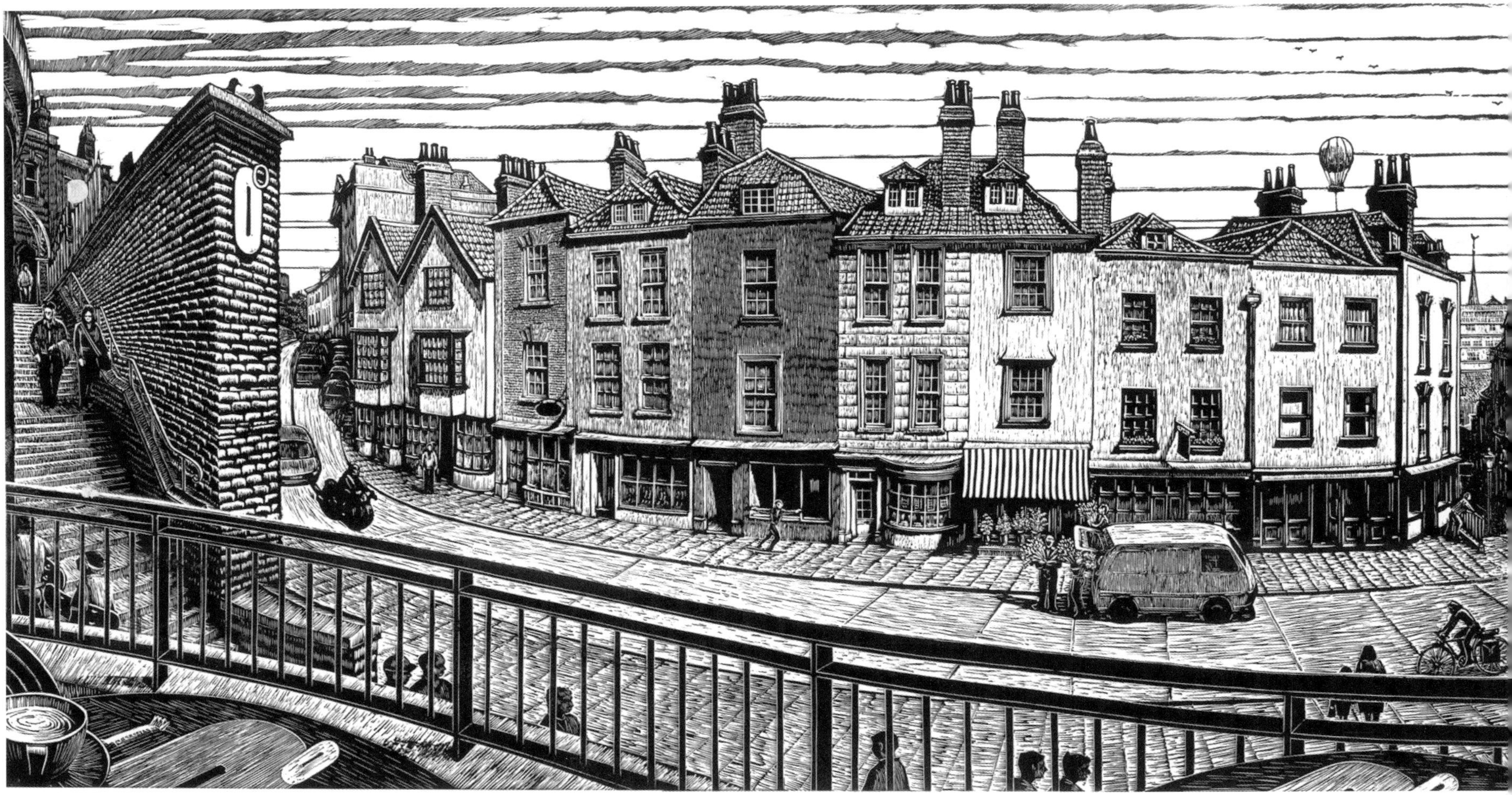

30 *Panorama from Zero Degrees, Colston Street*
reduced from 30 x 120cms (12 x 47ins)

As soon as this cleverly designed bar opened I began to sketch the new panorama it revealed from its balcony, looking across Colston Street to the top of Christmas Steps.

In order to include the whole sweep of buildings, I had to change my place each visit, moving from right to left along the balcony. The entire panorama cannot be seen from any one position there.

The engraving was selected for exhibition in the 2005 annual show of the Royal West of England Academy and was awarded the St Cuthbert's Mill prize.

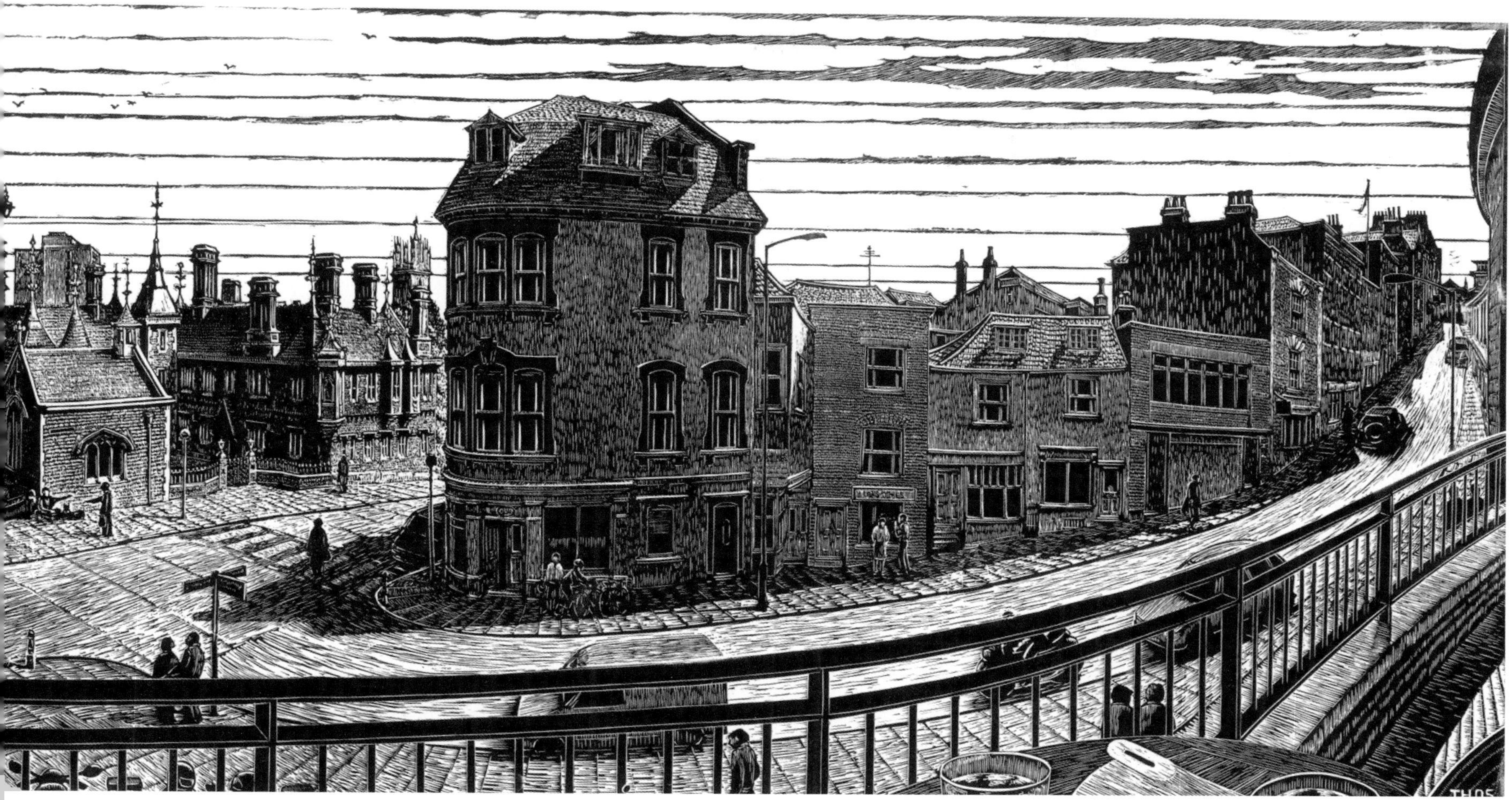

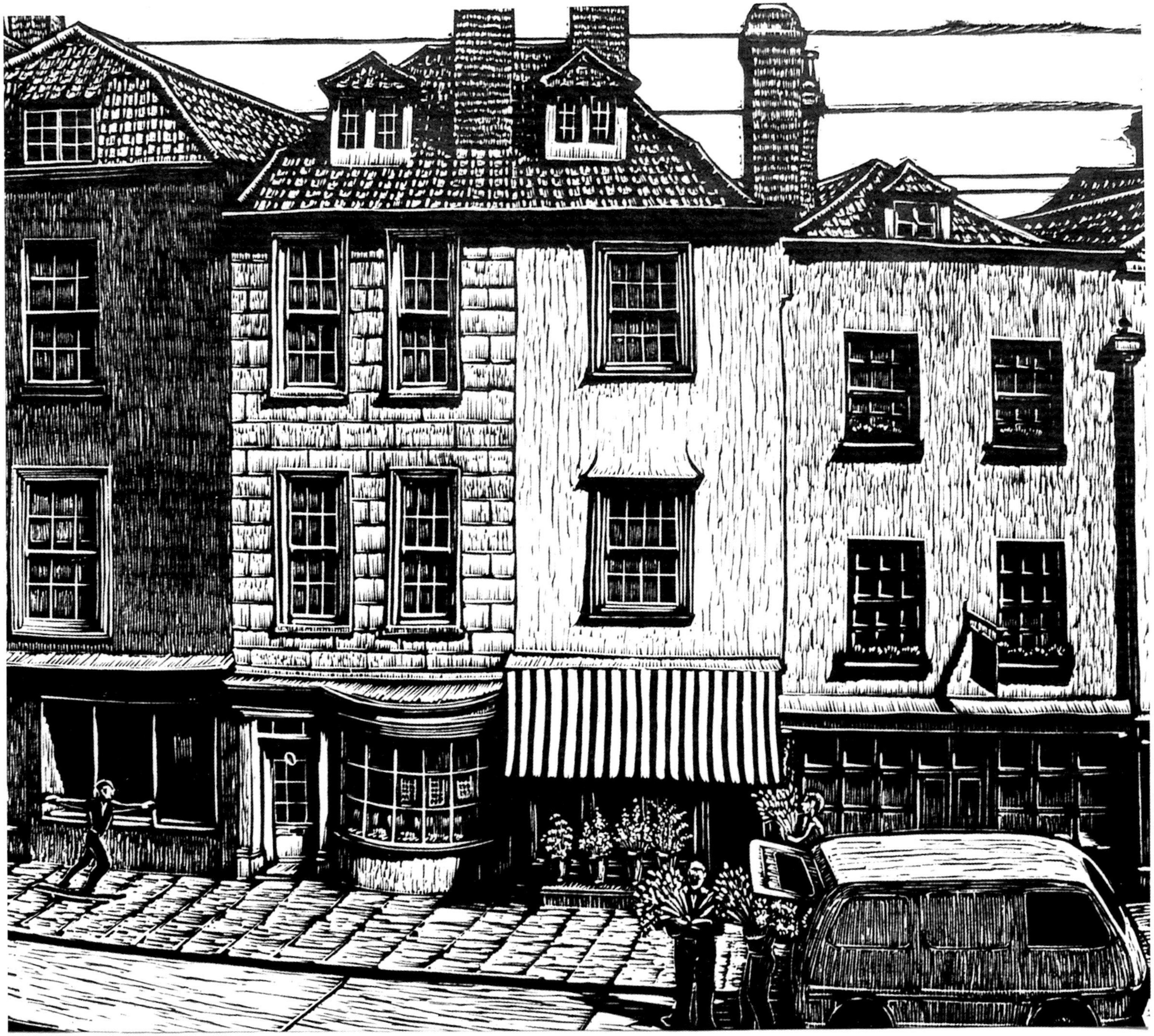

Two actual-size details from the previous plate:
Above: old shops at the top of Colston Street.
Opposite: the top of Christmas Steps.

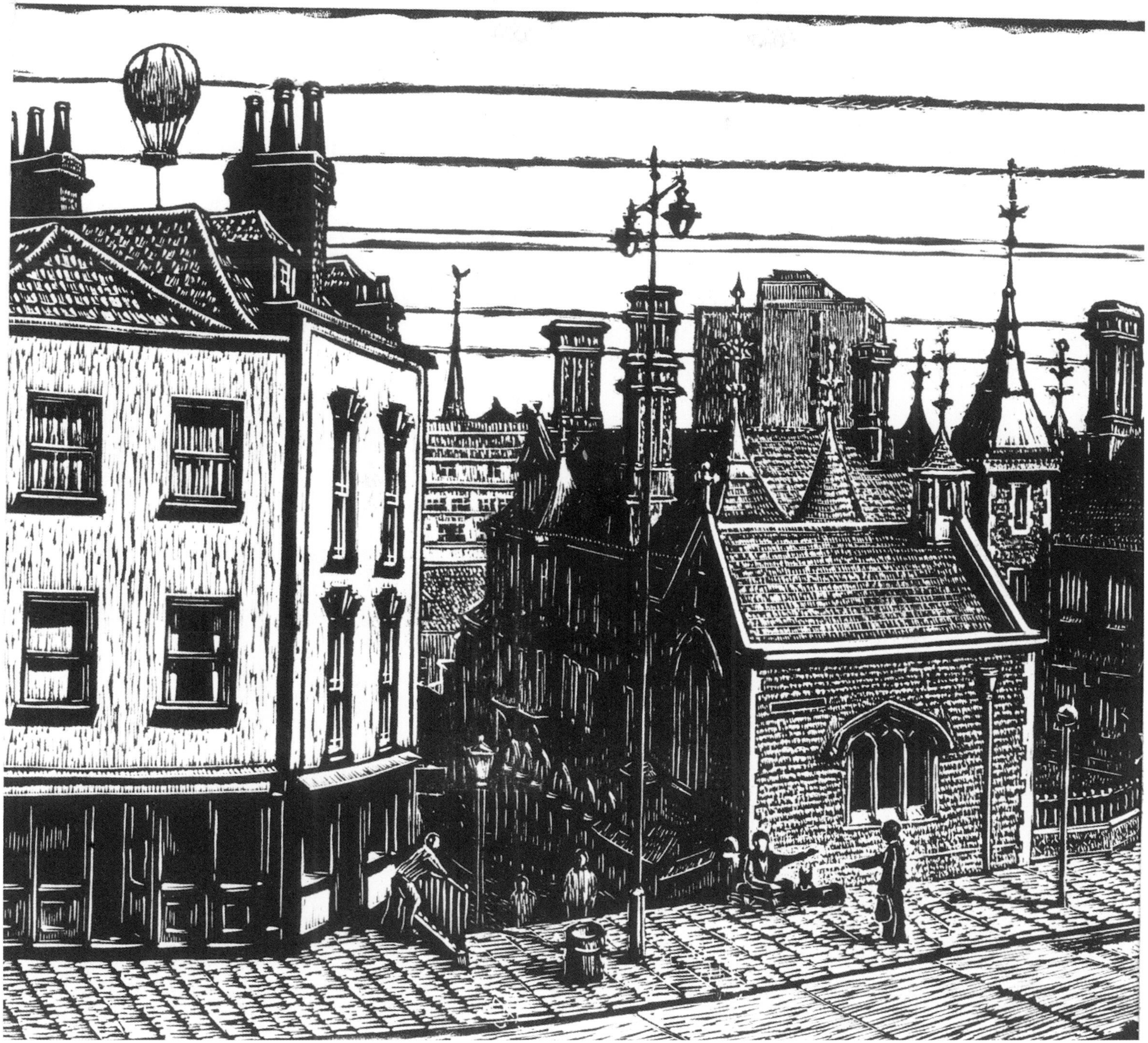

31 *Broad Street and St Michael's Hill*
reduced from 48 x 17cms (18¾ x 7ins)

After distributing begging letters up and down Broad Street (and suffering some rebuffs) a kind man let me into his top-floor apartment to get this view which I'd imagined must exist from what I had been able to glimpse down at street level.

St John's Church in the foreground is built over one of the old city gateways. The church in the background is St Michael's-on-the-Mount-Without and is now unused. It stands at the foot of St Michael's Hill.

I did this engraving as a companion piece to one I had done earlier of Christmas Steps and Park Row ('Panoramic Bristol' plate 46).

This whole area is full of interest. I return to it often and always find new compositions there.

Opposite: an actual-size detail from this engraving, showing St Michael's Hill.

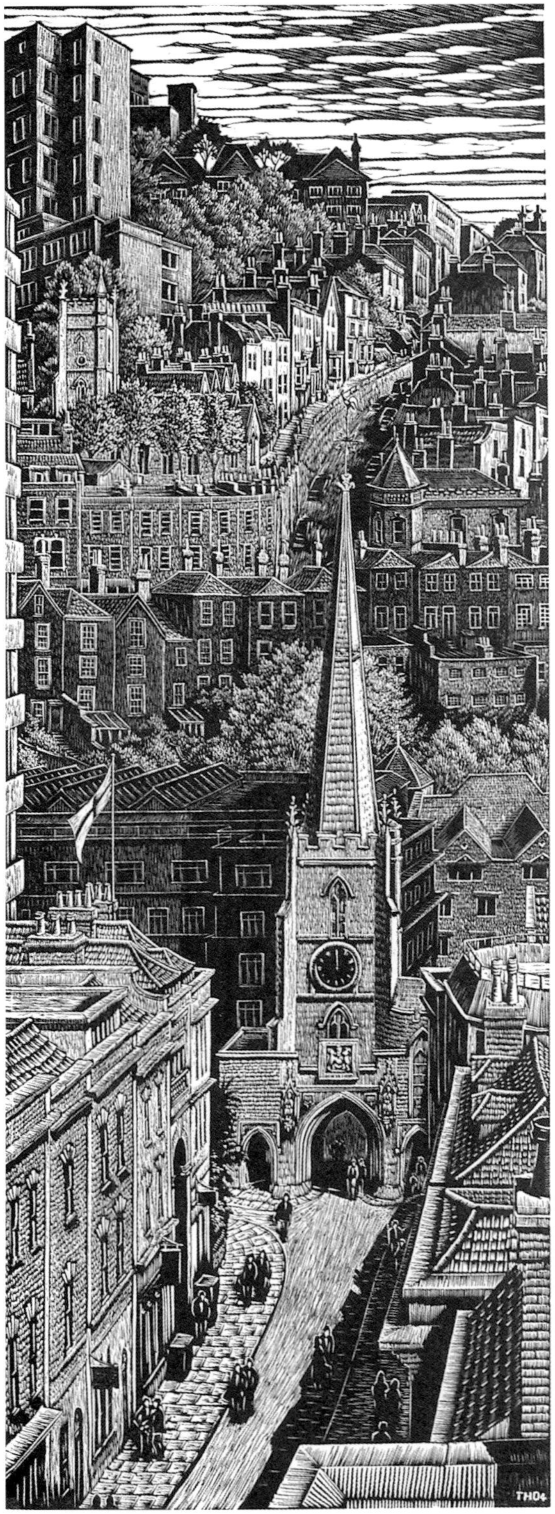

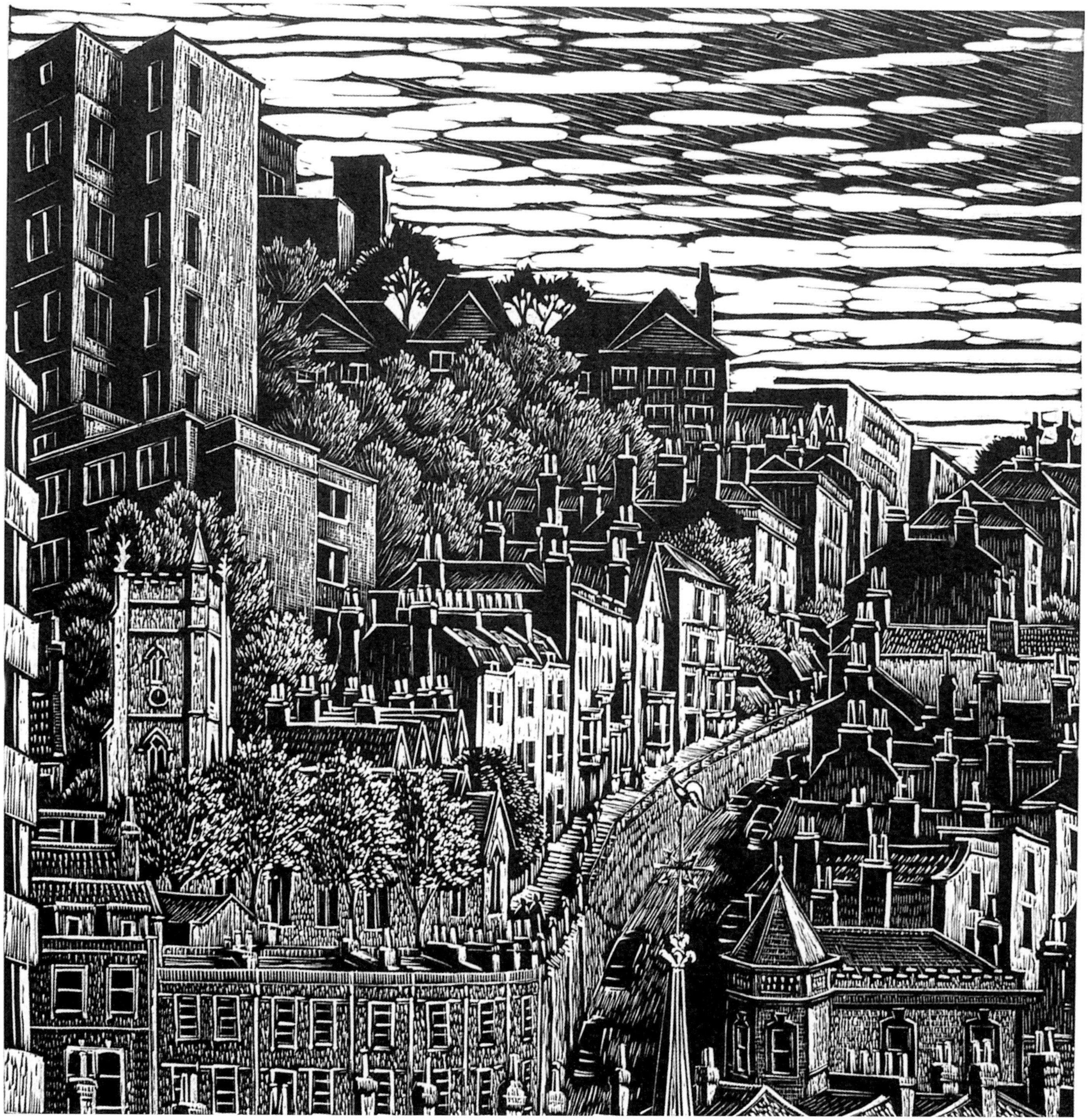

Clifton, Clifton Wood and Redland

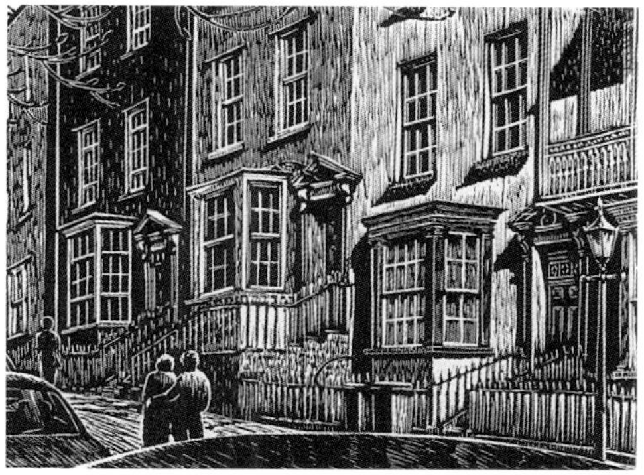

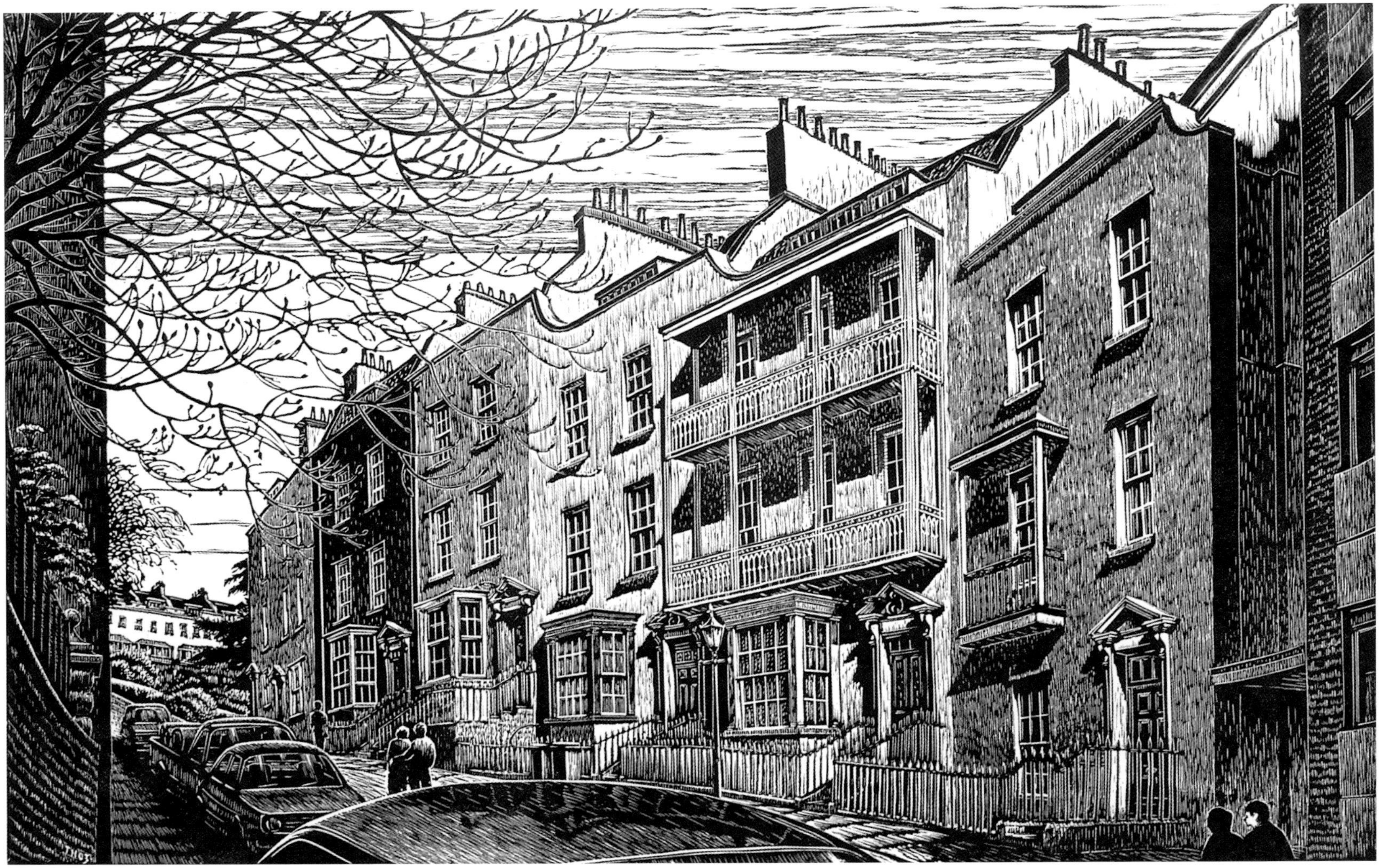

32 *Granby Hill, Clifton*
reduced from 22.5 x 37cms (9 x 14½ ins)

This was a commission from the owner of one of the houses in this steep but very attractive street. The elegant wrought-iron balconies and bay windows were a challenge to engrave.

Opposite: actual-size detail from this engraving.

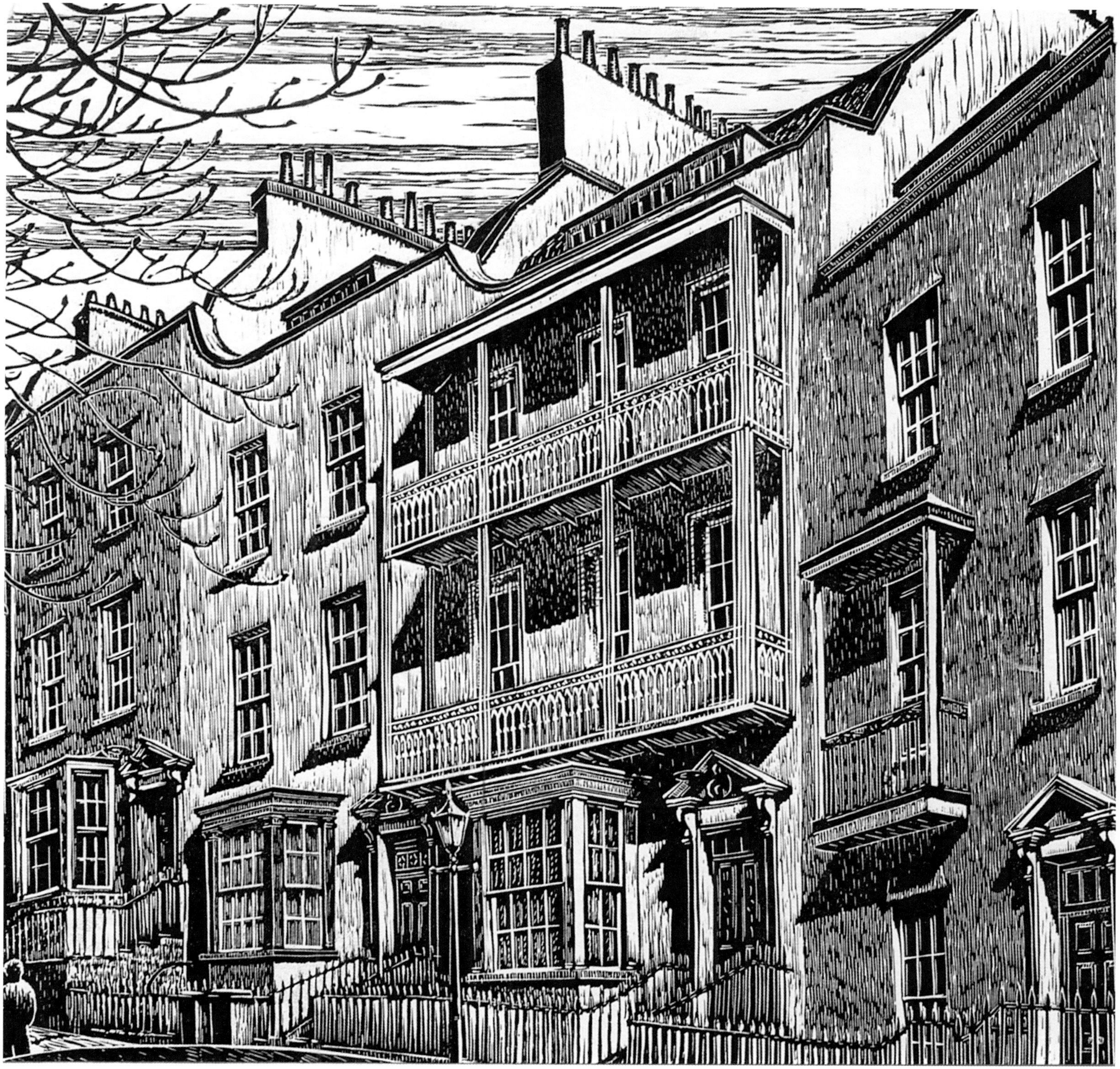

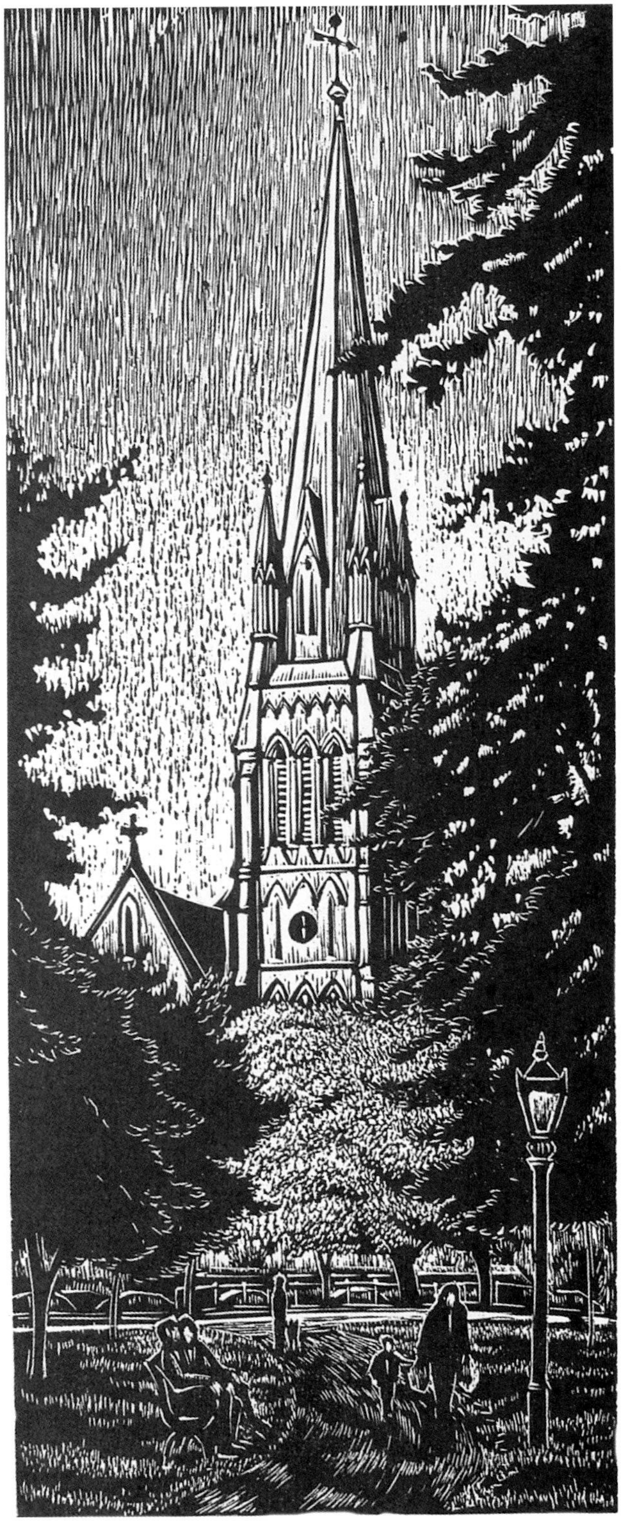

33 *Christchurch, Clifton*
actual size

I've always enjoyed the way this spire comes into view between the trees as you walk towards it across the green opposite. This was an evening view, drawn in the autumn.

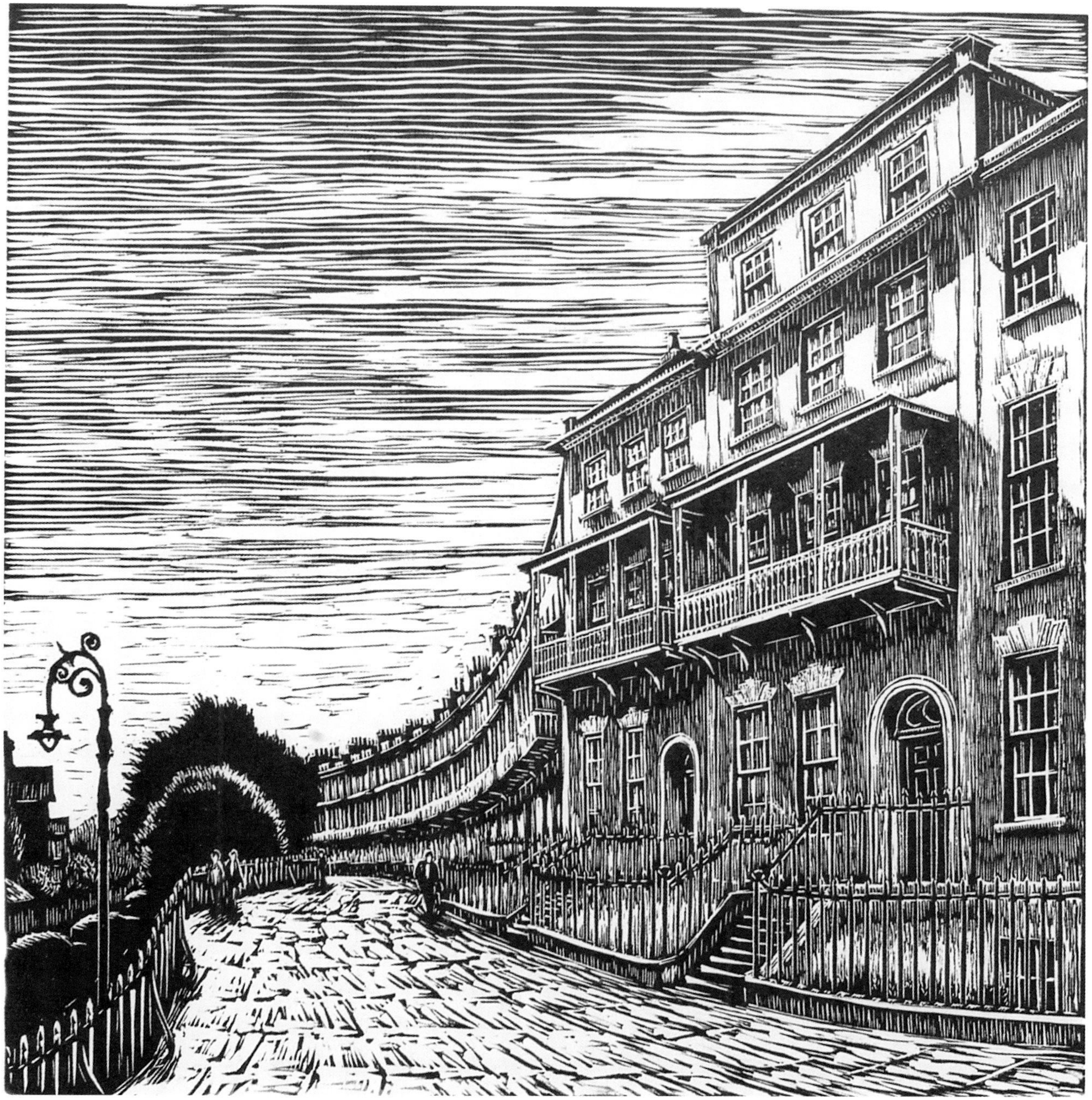

34 *Royal York Crescent, Clifton*
actual size

I was commissioned to do a water-colour of this end of the crescent in 2005. I used the same sketch as the starting point for this engraving. The dramatic diagonal sweep of the buildings seen from this angle appealed to me. The square format emphasises this.

35 Right: ***White Hart Steps, Clifton Wood*** *summer*
reduced from 21.5 x 7cms ($8^1/_4$ x $2^3/_4$ins)

36 Far right: ***the cottages from Hotwell Road***
actual size

These steps manage to retain their charm despite the encroachment of developments on Hotwell Road and on the nearby dockside.

I like the unfolding rhythms and textures of the area viewed from above. It reminds me of certain Japanese 'pillar prints' I've seen in the British Museum where the viewer is invited to go on a journey within the composition. I've produced many engravings where this is the basic intention.

The simple stacked forms of the cottages are more apparent from Hotwell Road.

We are fortunate in Bristol to have interesting nooks and crannies like this remaining so close to the city centre. They need guarding, though.

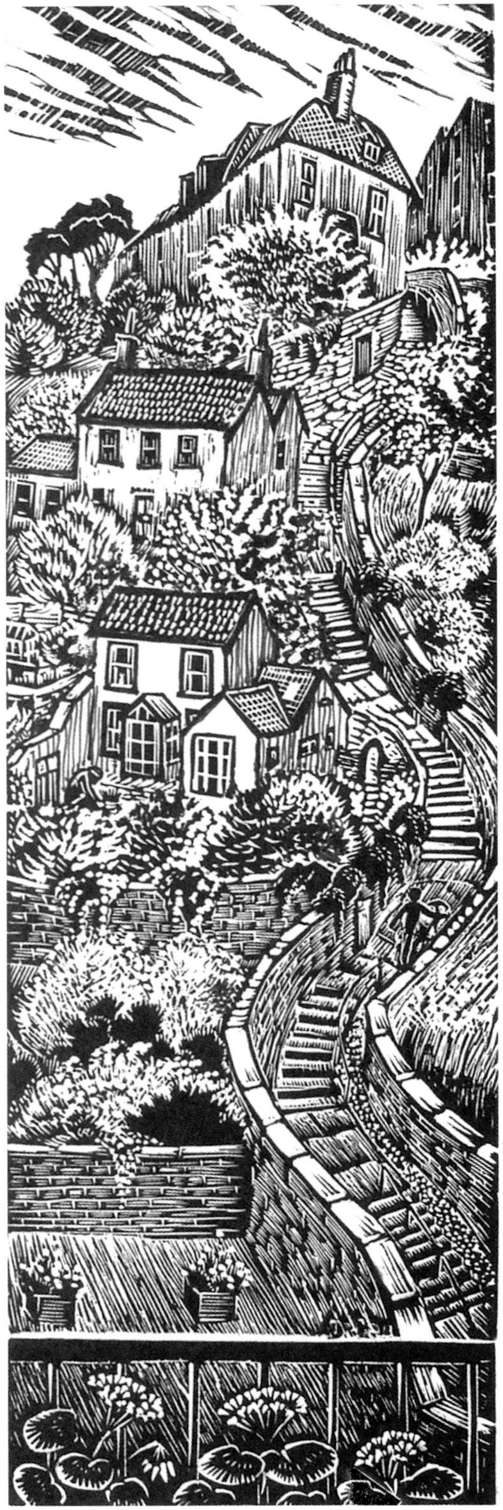

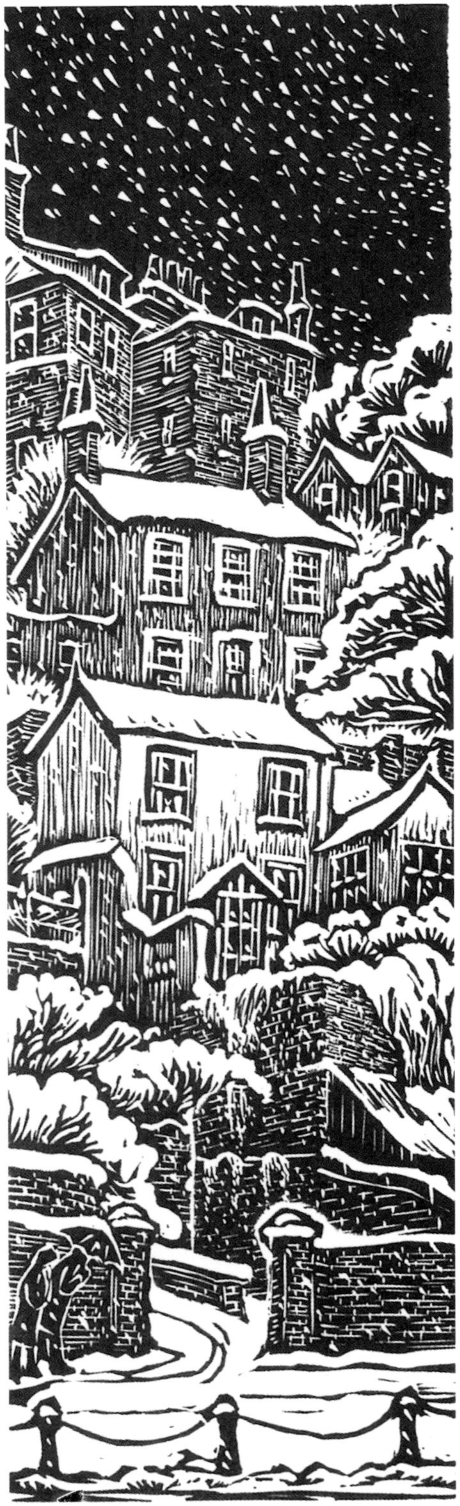

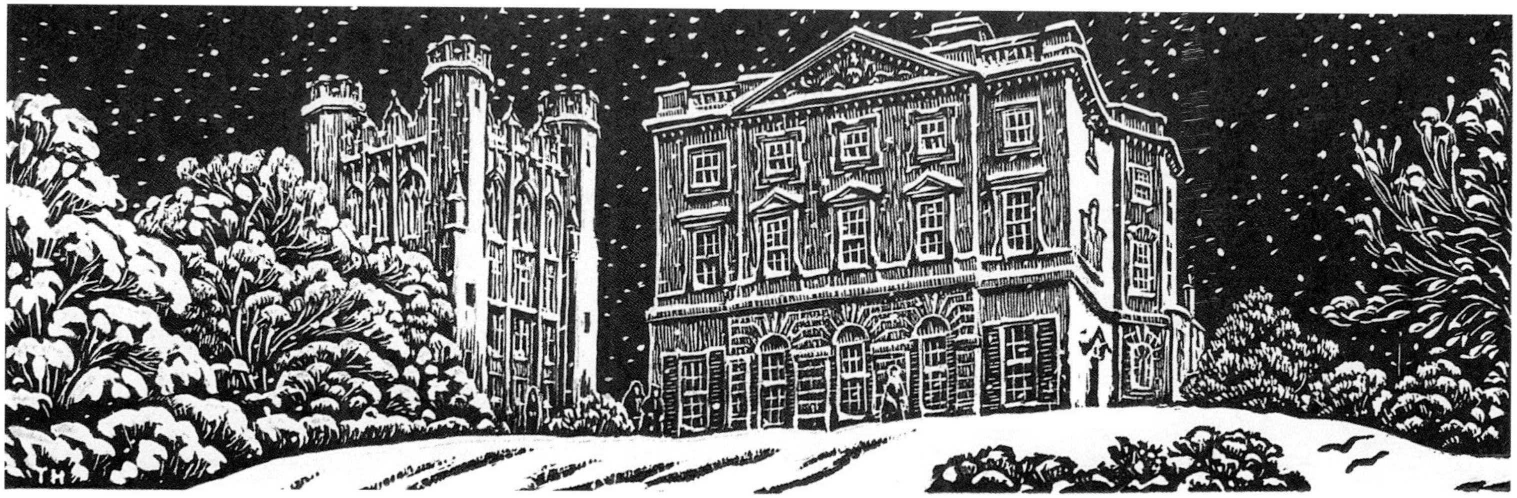

37 *Royal Fort House and the Physics Building, University of Bristol*
actual size

This engraving was done for the University to use as a card design at Christmas, 2005. The sketch was actually done in the height of summer so imaginary snow was required once more.

These two buildings make attractive partners and I tried to find a composition which would show this, along with a hint of the beautiful gardens which surround them.

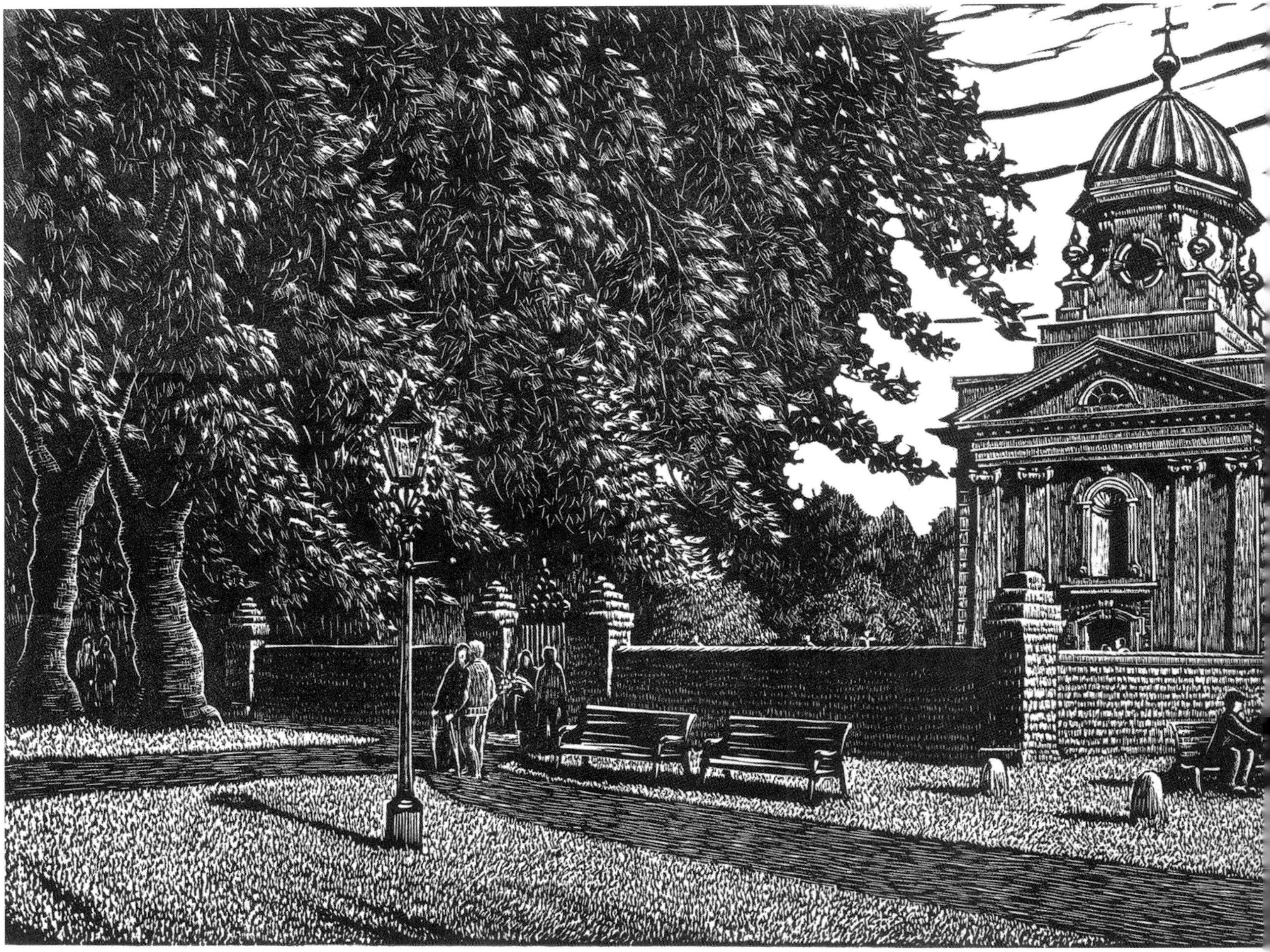

38 *Redland Church and Redland Green*
reduced from 17 x 48cms (7 x 18$^{3/4}$ ins)

I was asked to do this engraving in 2004. Profits from sales of some of the original prints were donated to a restoration fund for the Thomas Paty wood-carvings round the altar. The graceful building is surrounded by a most interesting group of trees and I took pleasure in trying to suggest the different types of foliage.

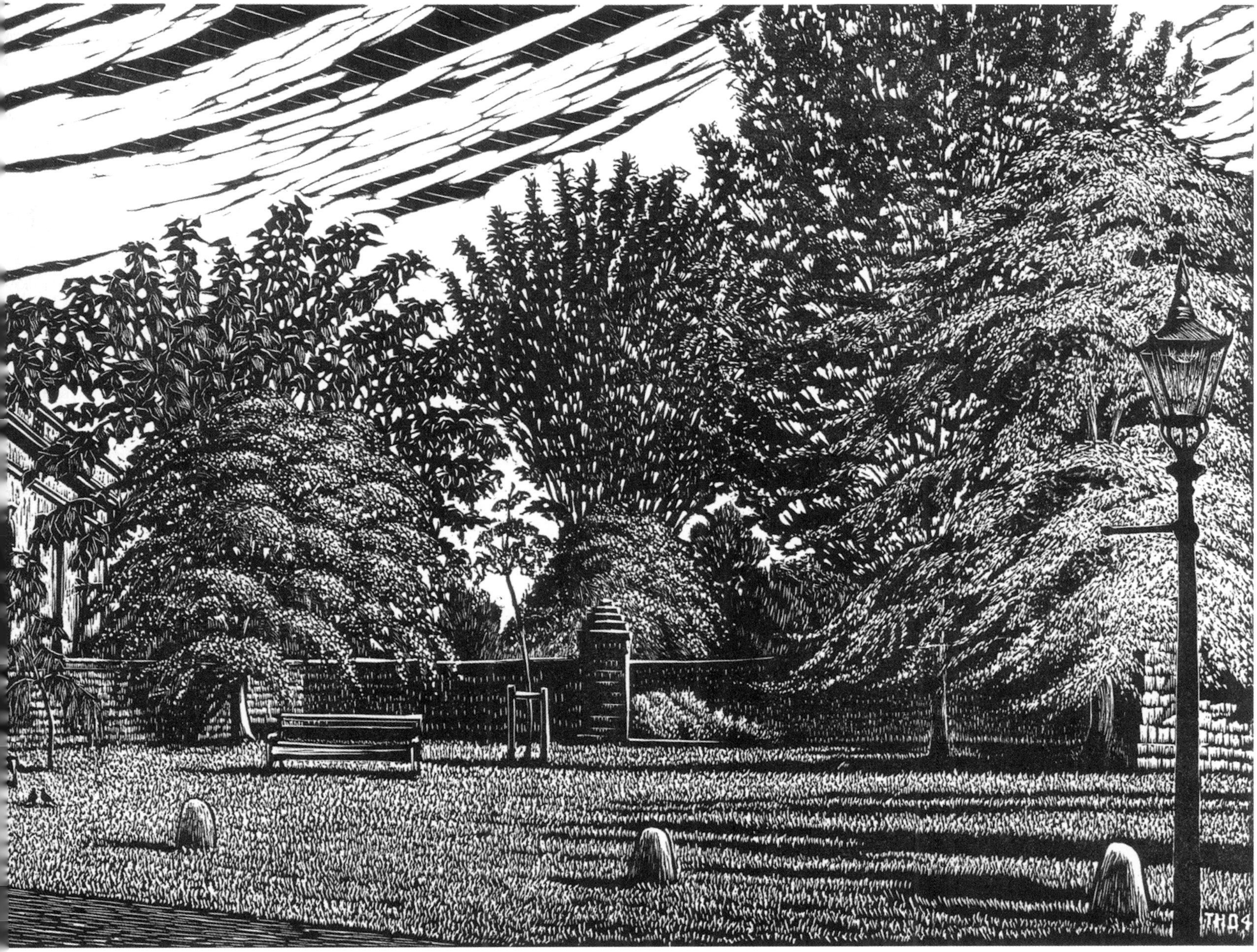

A Theatrical Interlude

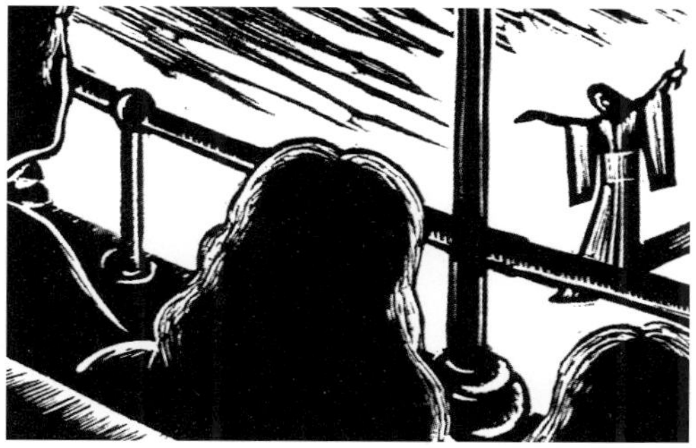

I want to conclude this section with a small set of prints of a well loved Bristol interior: that of the Bristol Hippodrome.

I've spent many life-enhancing evenings there over nearly 40 years in the city, mainly thanks to Welsh National Opera who gave me my introduction to, and education in, that art form during their annual visits here.

There have also been some extraordinary productions of musicals and occasional one-off concerts by gifted individual performers, too. (Will I ever recover from Miss Eartha Kitt singing 'I Can't Give You Anything But Love, Baby' right at me, sitting in the front row of the stalls?)

The theatre was designed by Frank Matcham who also designed the Coliseum, London and influenced the design of the Lyceum, Sheffield, which I remember visiting in my childhood.

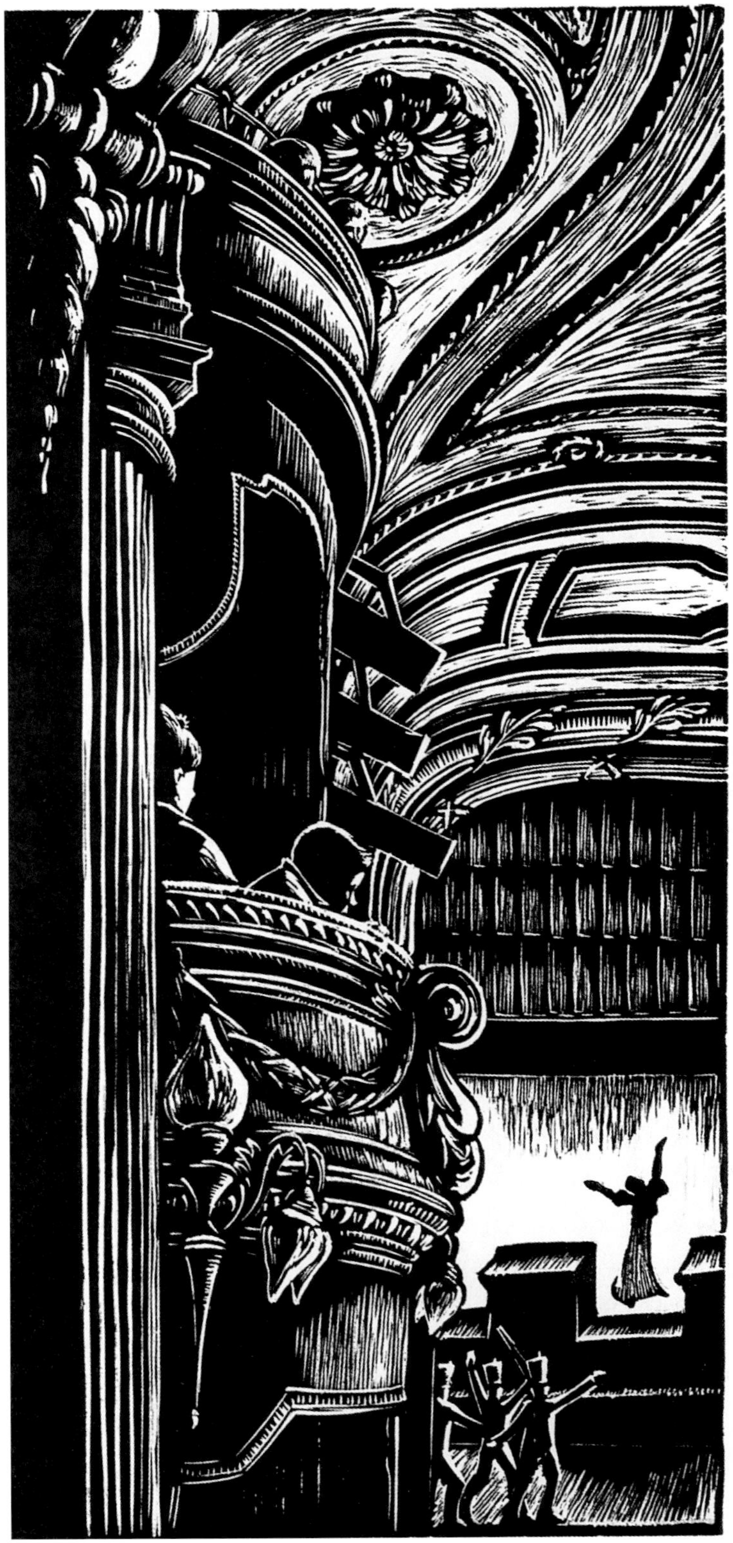

39 *The Final Moment [1]* **Tosca**
actual size

The heroine leaps off the battlements of Castel Sant Angelo in the thrilling close of Puccini's opera.

I've always like these oblique views along the ornate boxes, even though one gets a very restricted view of the stage when sitting in them.

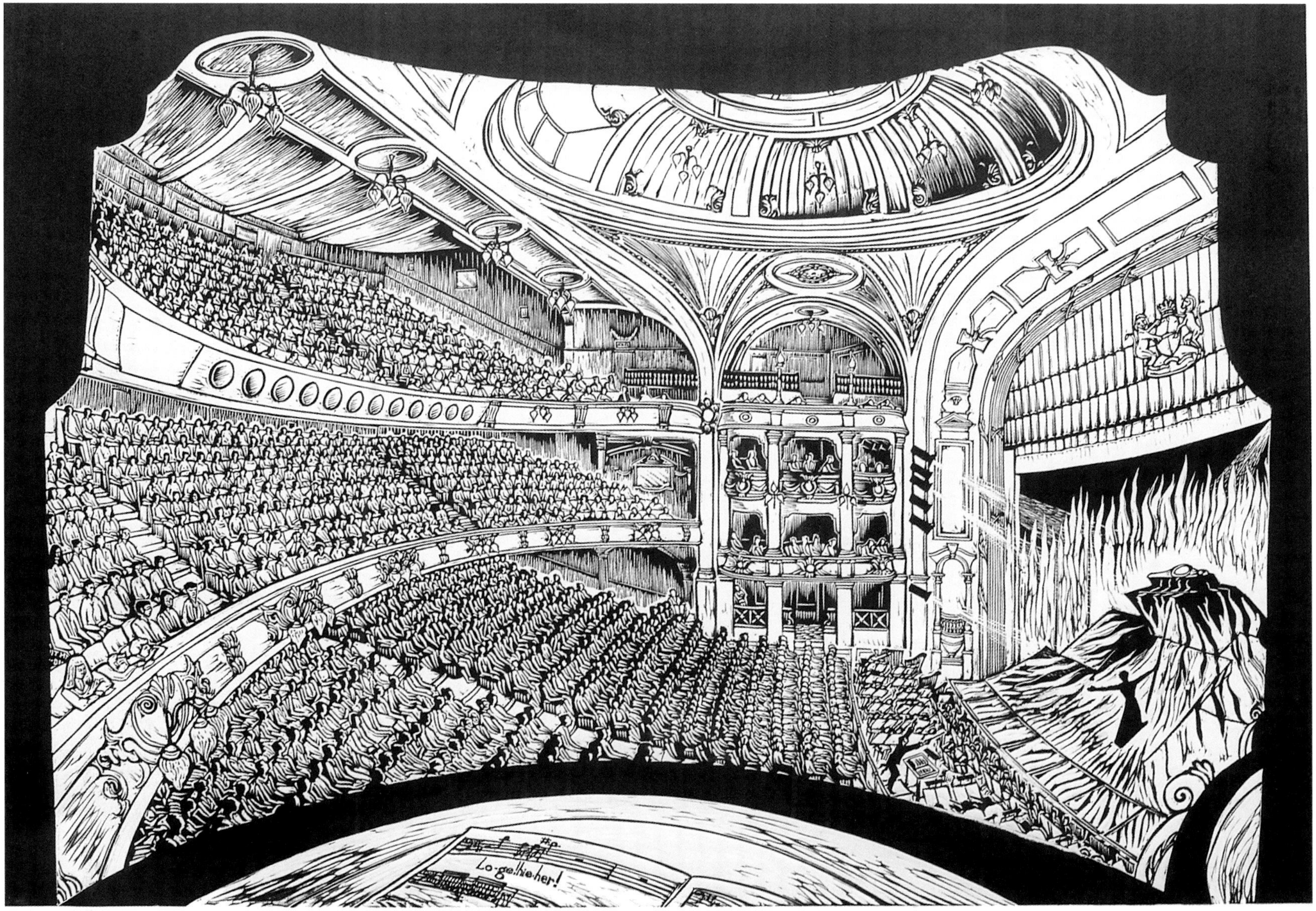

40 *Wotan's Farewell (*Die Walküre *Act III)*
reduced from 36 x 52cms (14 x 20½ ins)

I drew this sitting in a side box, on my own, with a battery-operated reading lamp clipped to my sketch-pad, during a painful (and ill-attended) rock musical. The view of the entire theatre was a joy to try and record.

This is my own, imagined production on-stage showing that most profoundly moving moment when Wotan bids farewell to his favourite daughter, sends her to sleep, and surrounds her with magic fire.

I have also done coloured versions of this design using additional blocks printed underneath. It is one of a series of studies of opera houses I have made, usually with scenes from Wagner operas on stage.

41 *The Final Moment [2]* **Madame Butterfly**
actual size

Poor little Butterfly reaches her end. I drew this, many years ago, standing in 'the gods' but made this engraving from the sketch only quite recently.

(An artist should never throw anything away)

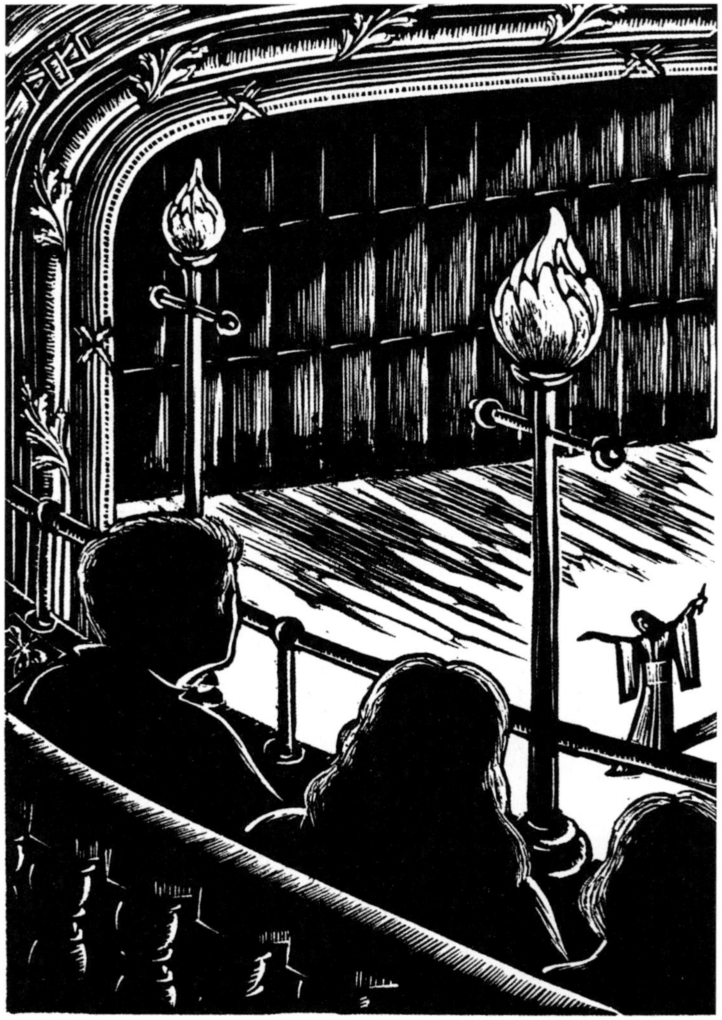

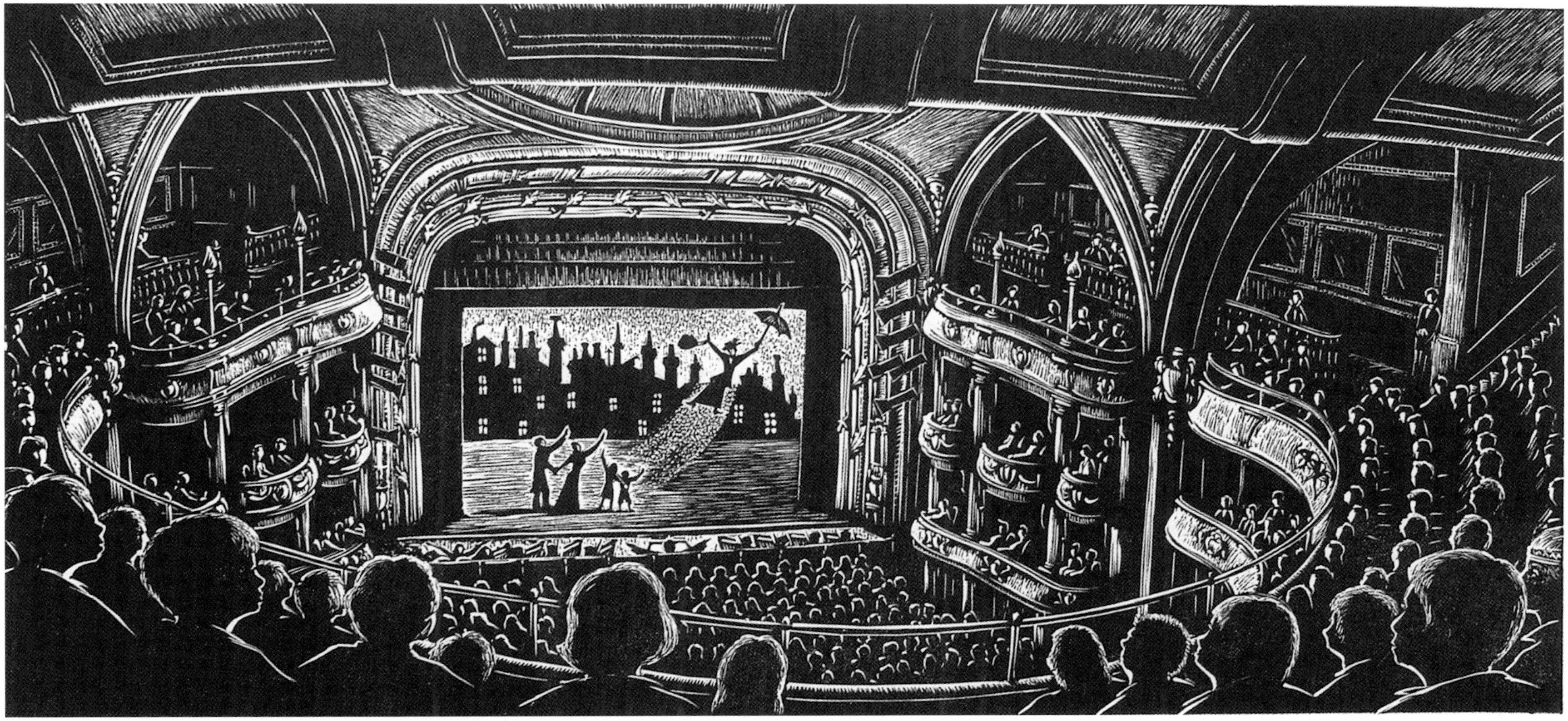

42 *World premiere of the musical* **Mary Poppins** *Bristol Hippodrome 2005*
reduced from 14 x 32cms ($5\frac{1}{2}$ x $12\frac{1}{2}$ ins)

I just loved this! It was intelligent, moving and performed by an incredibly talented cast.

This is the moment, right at the end, when Miss Poppins takes her breath-taking flight across the whole auditorium to land just to the left of where I drew this view.

I was aiming to capture the way the glow from the stage illuminates the theatre and gives everyone in the audience their own little halo.

I re-engraved the sliver containing the orchestra three times over before I was satisfied with it.

And Beyond...

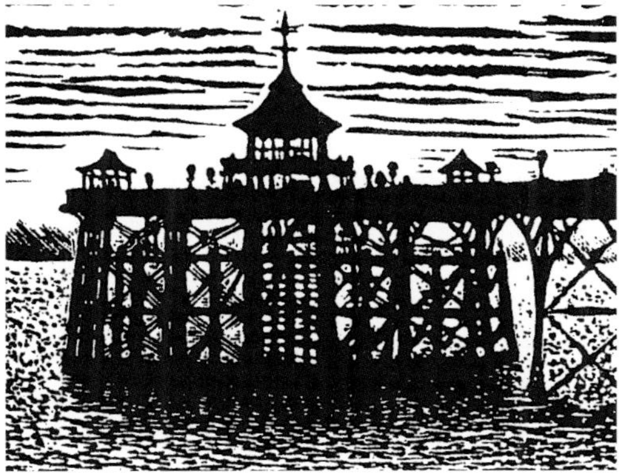

This final section is devoted to a selection of prints drawn from some of the places of interest which can be found within a few miles of the city.

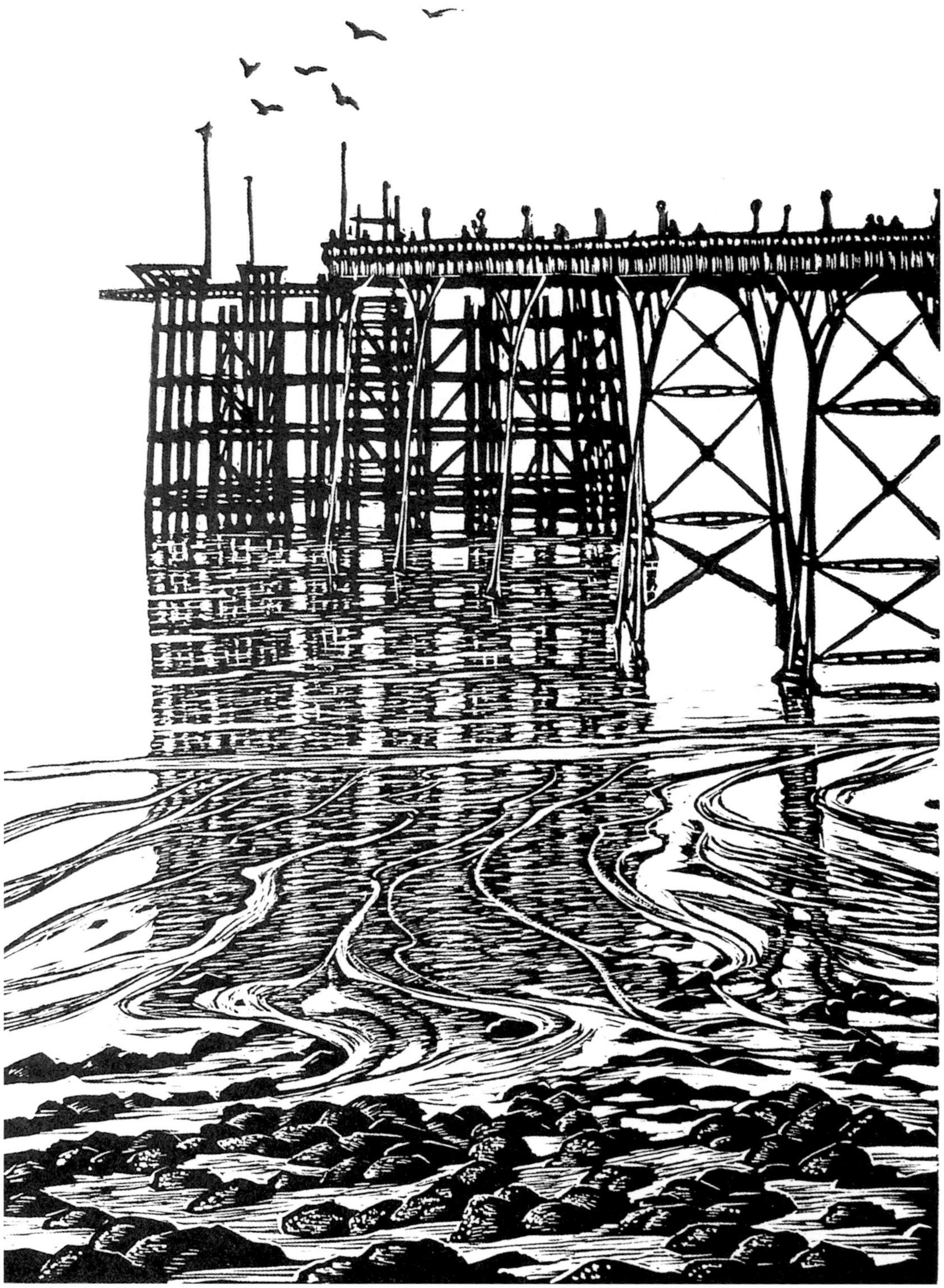

43 *Clevedon Pier during restoration: Low Tide*
actual size

I drew this some years ago before the admirable restoration got under way. The engraving is a recent product, though.

The abstract design created by the reflections of the pier in the wet sand as the tide went out was fascinating. My task was to try and convey both the flat horizontal plane of the water and the reflections which seemed to go vertically down into it.

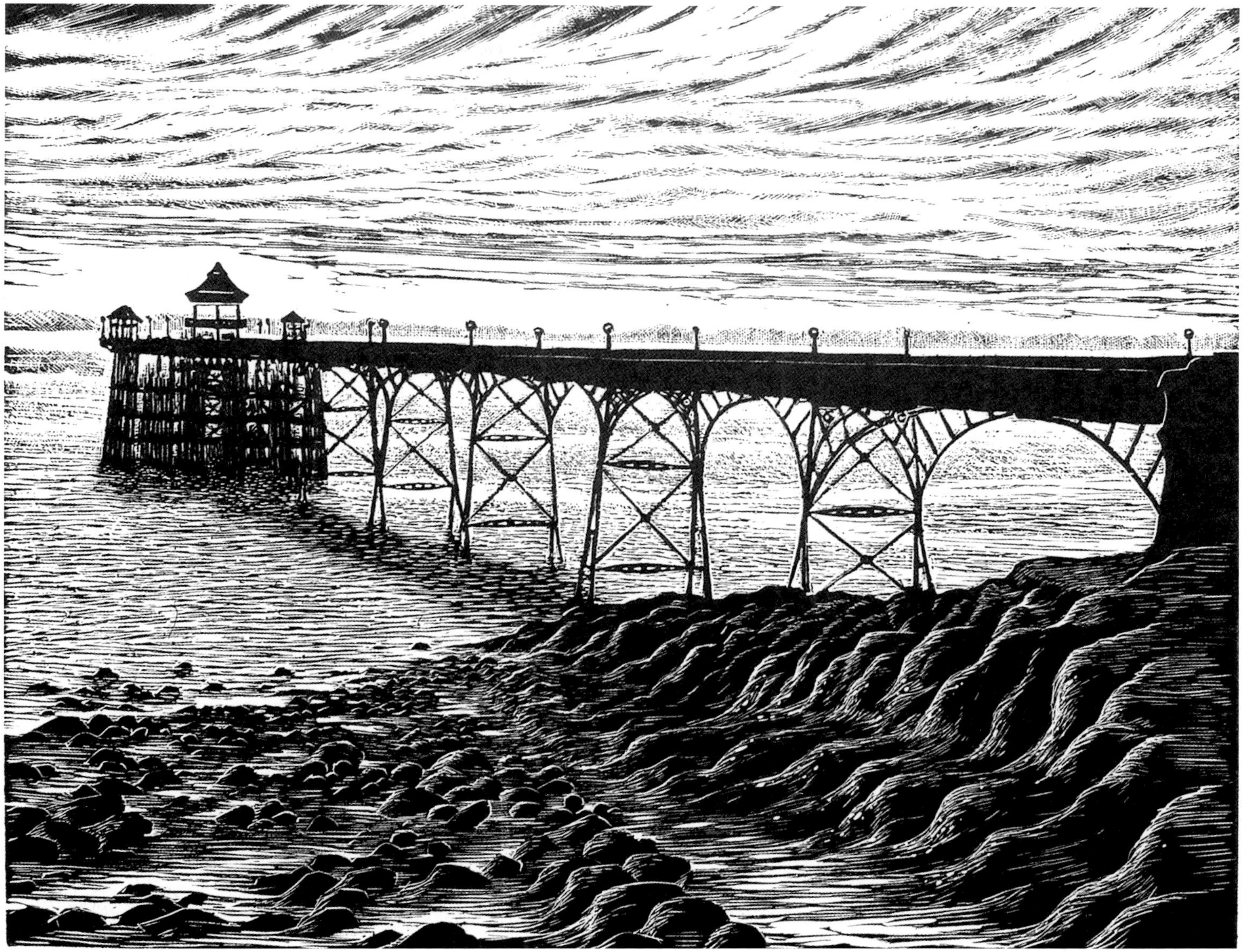

44 Clevedon Pier soon after restoration
actual size

This was engraved in the early 1990s soon after the pier was restored and opened to the public once more. I made a series of engravings of other piers following this, including the ill-fated West Pier, Brighton.

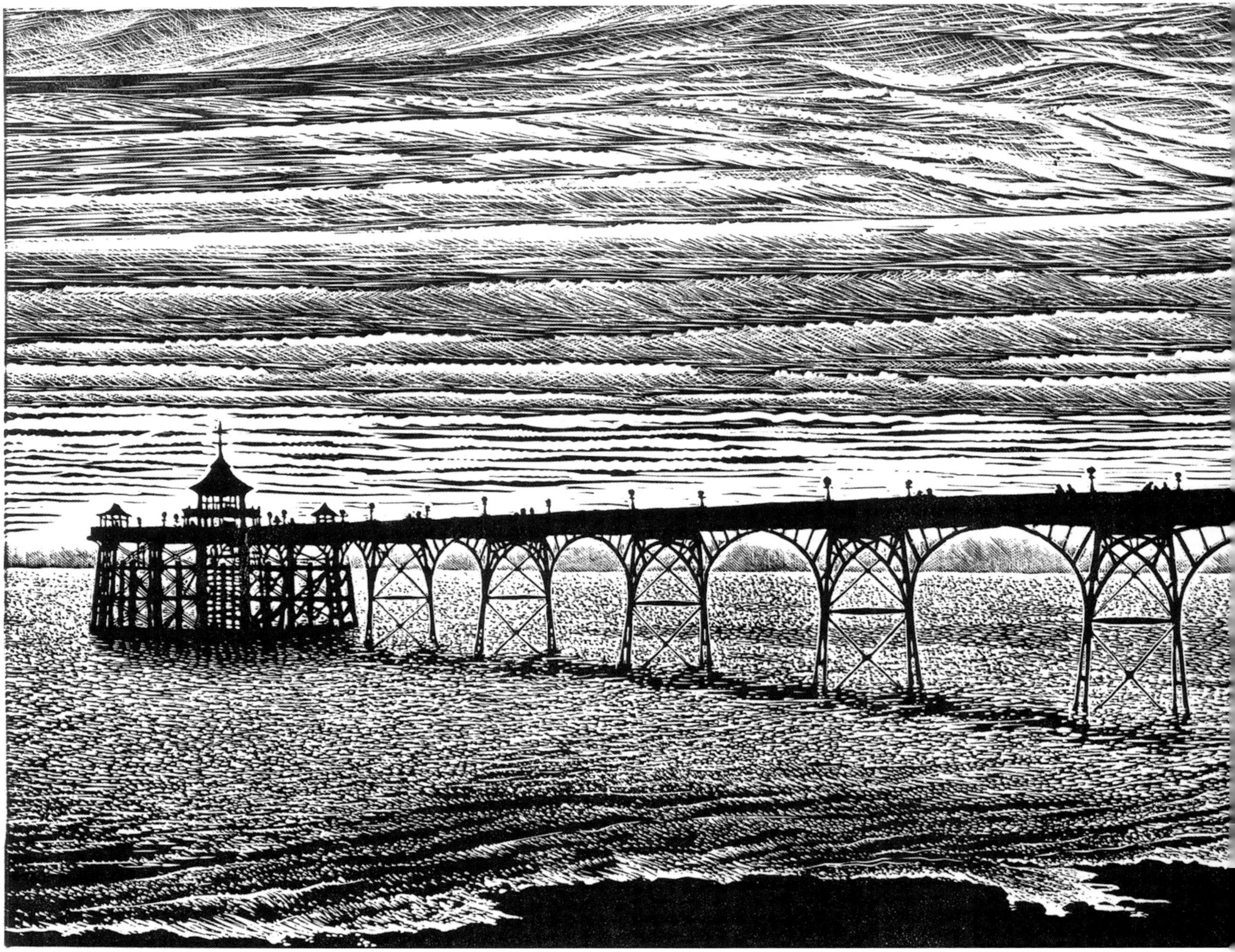

45 *Stormy day, Clevedon Pier*
reduced from 17 x 48cms (7 x 18¾ ins)

This was engraved the year after my first attempt. I saw it with a churning sky overhead and a biting gale blowing.

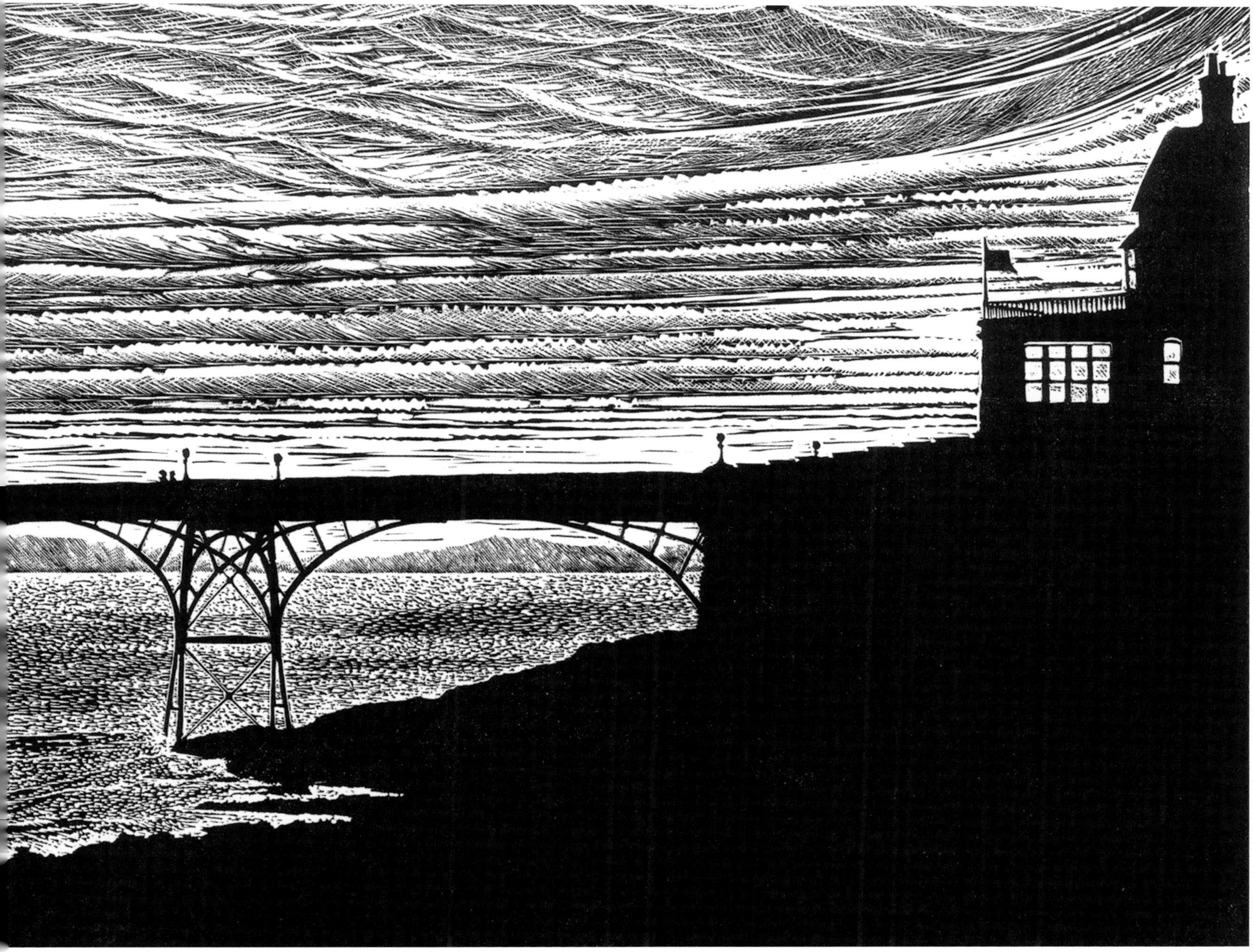

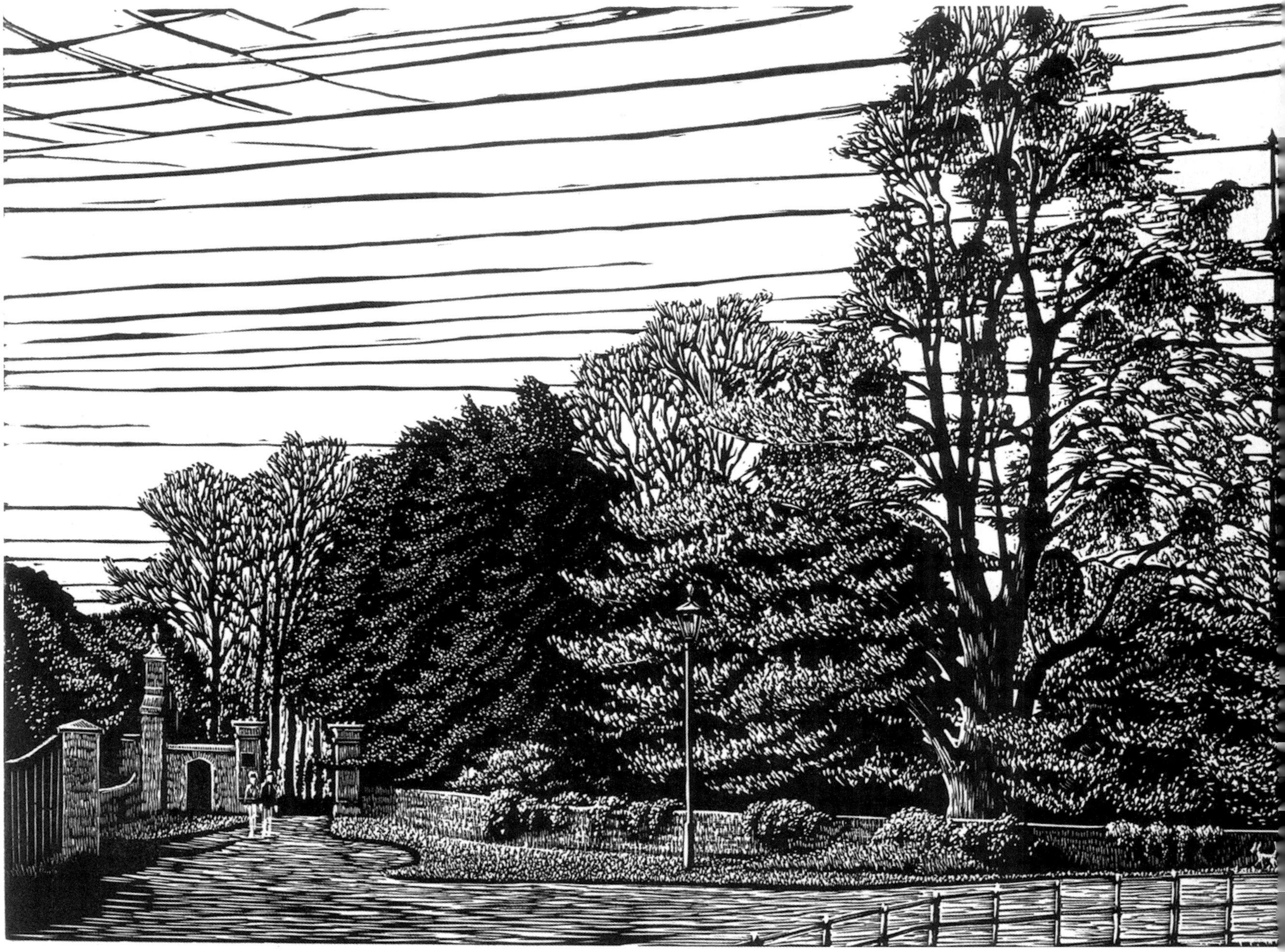

46 ***St Mary's Church, Thornbury***
reduced from 17 x 48cms (7 x 18¾ ins)

In 2004, I was invited to put on the inaugural exhibition at the magnificent new art gallery at Castle School, Thornbury. I produced this set of four prints specially for that exhibition.

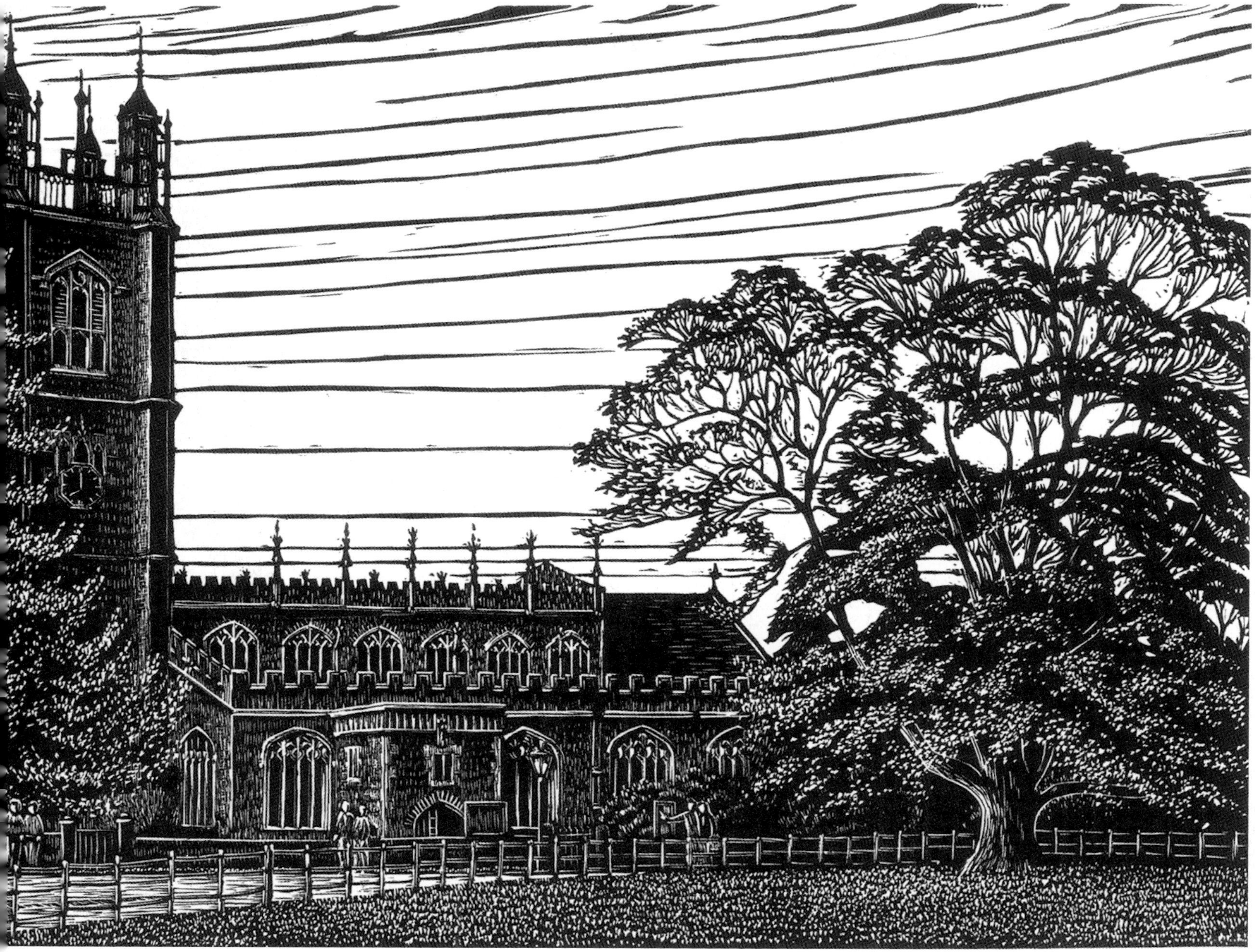

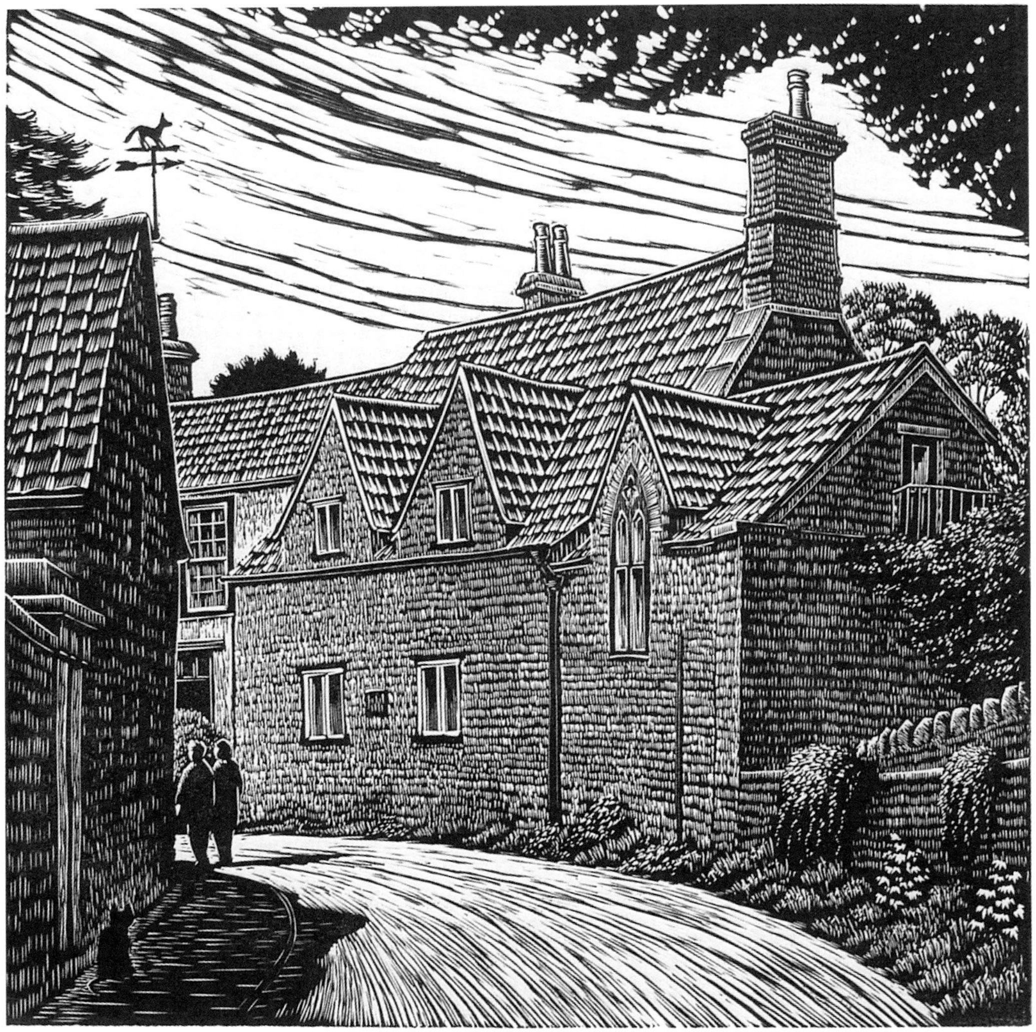

47 *The Old Grammar School, Thornbury*
reduced from 20cms square (8 x 8 ins)

Thornbury is full of quaint scenes like this, near the school. Many artists have been attracted to the place over the years.

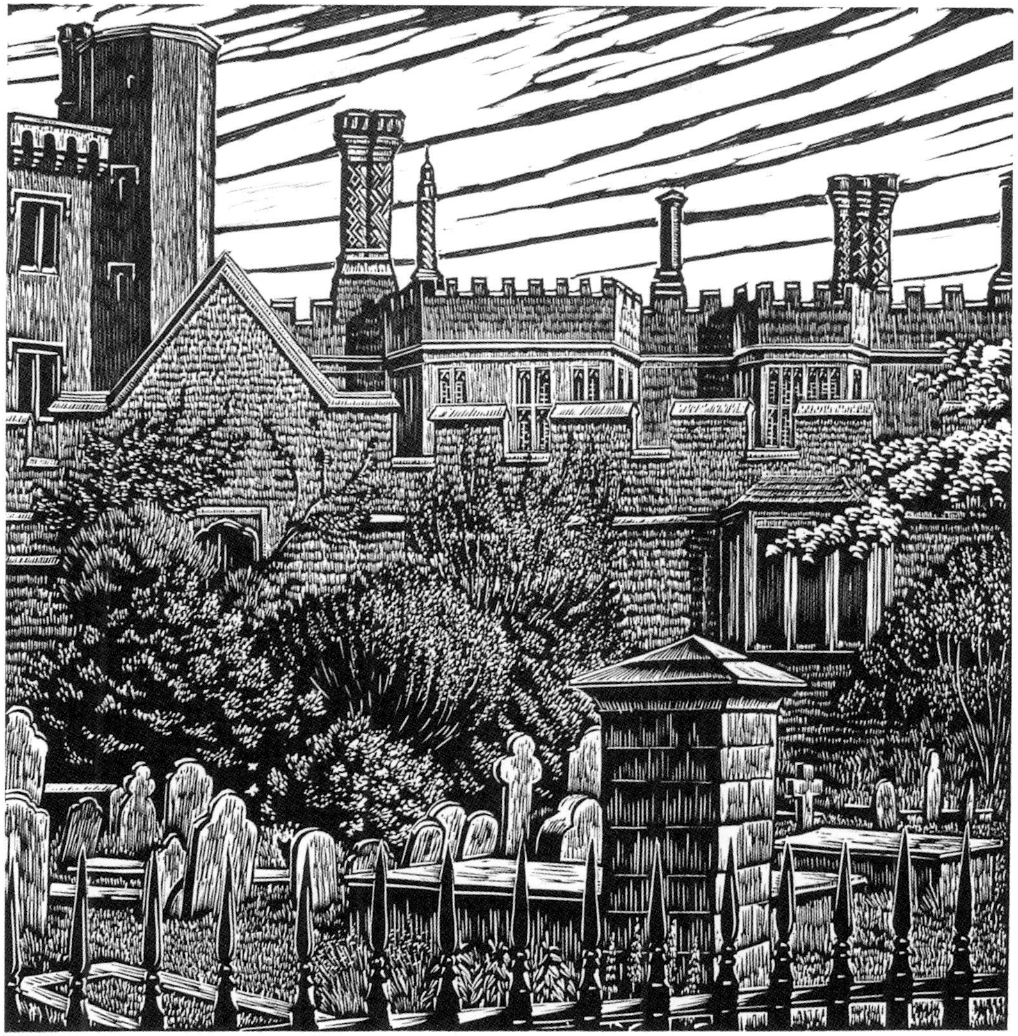

48 *Churchyard and Castle, Thornbury*
reduced from 20cms square (8 x 8 ins)

Overlapping layers of space and varied textures attracted me to this view.

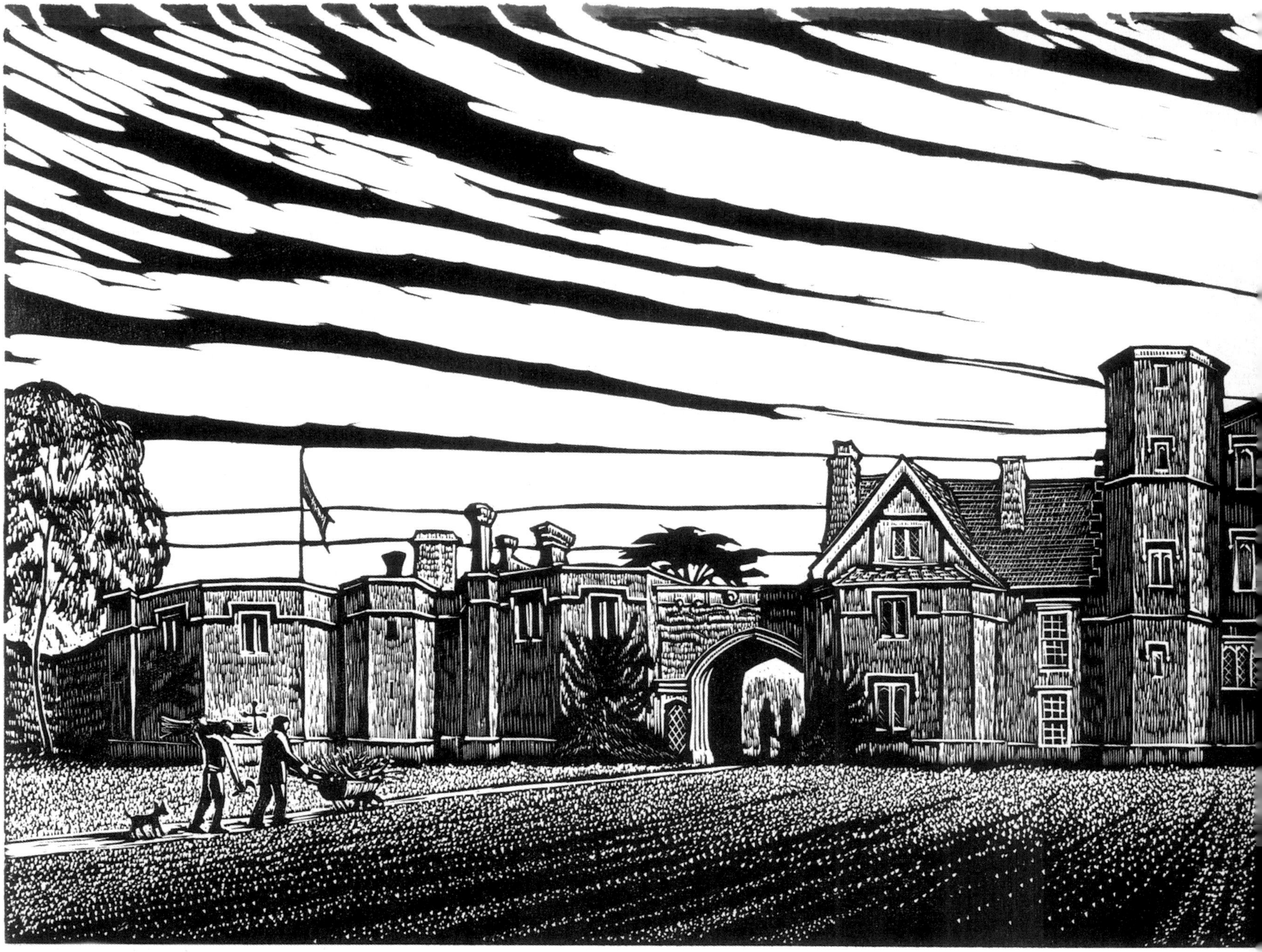

49 *Entrance to Thornbury Castle*
reduced from 17 x 48cms (7 x 18¾ ins)

The dramatic build-up of shapes from left to right was what I was trying to emphasise.

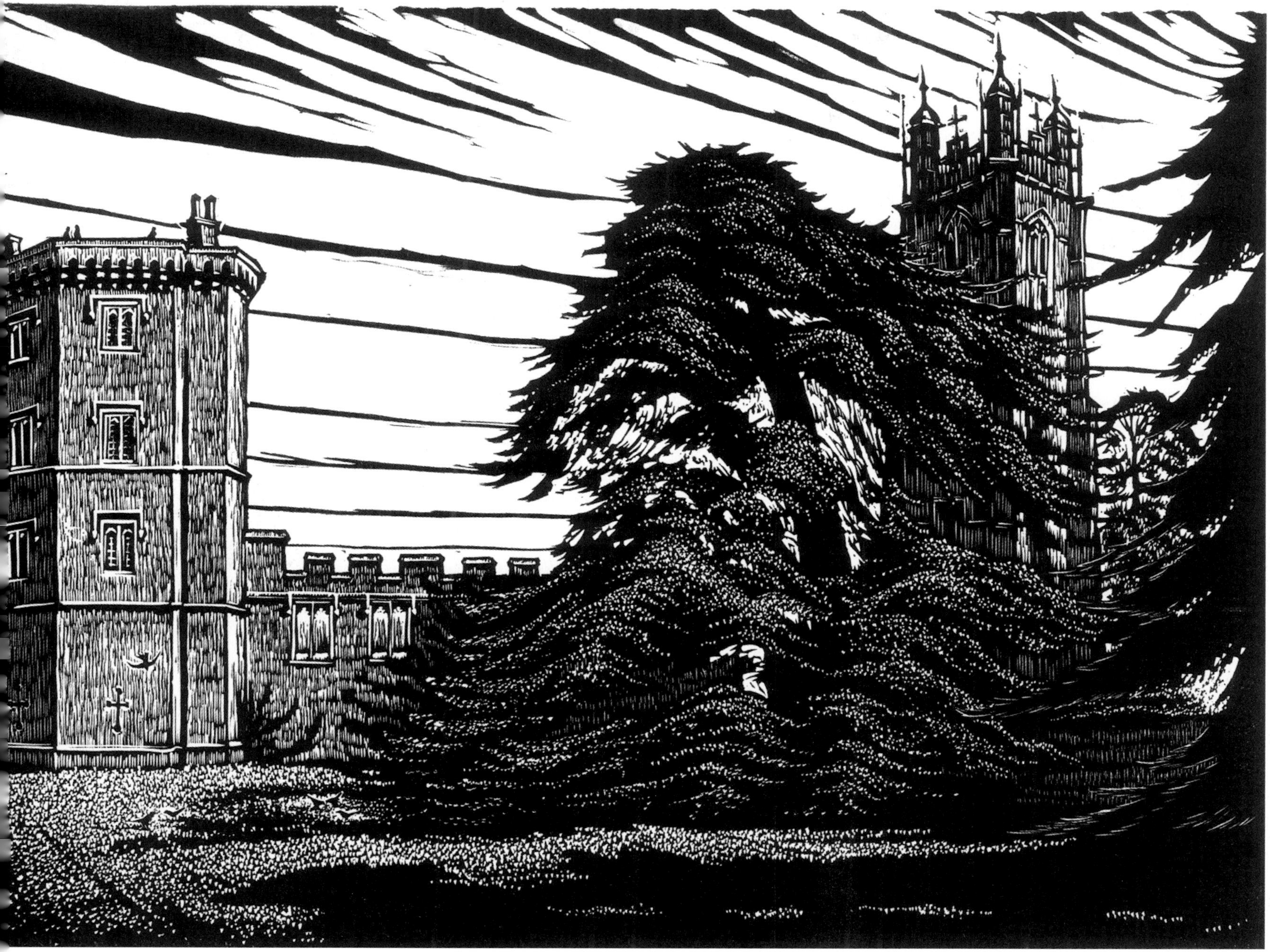

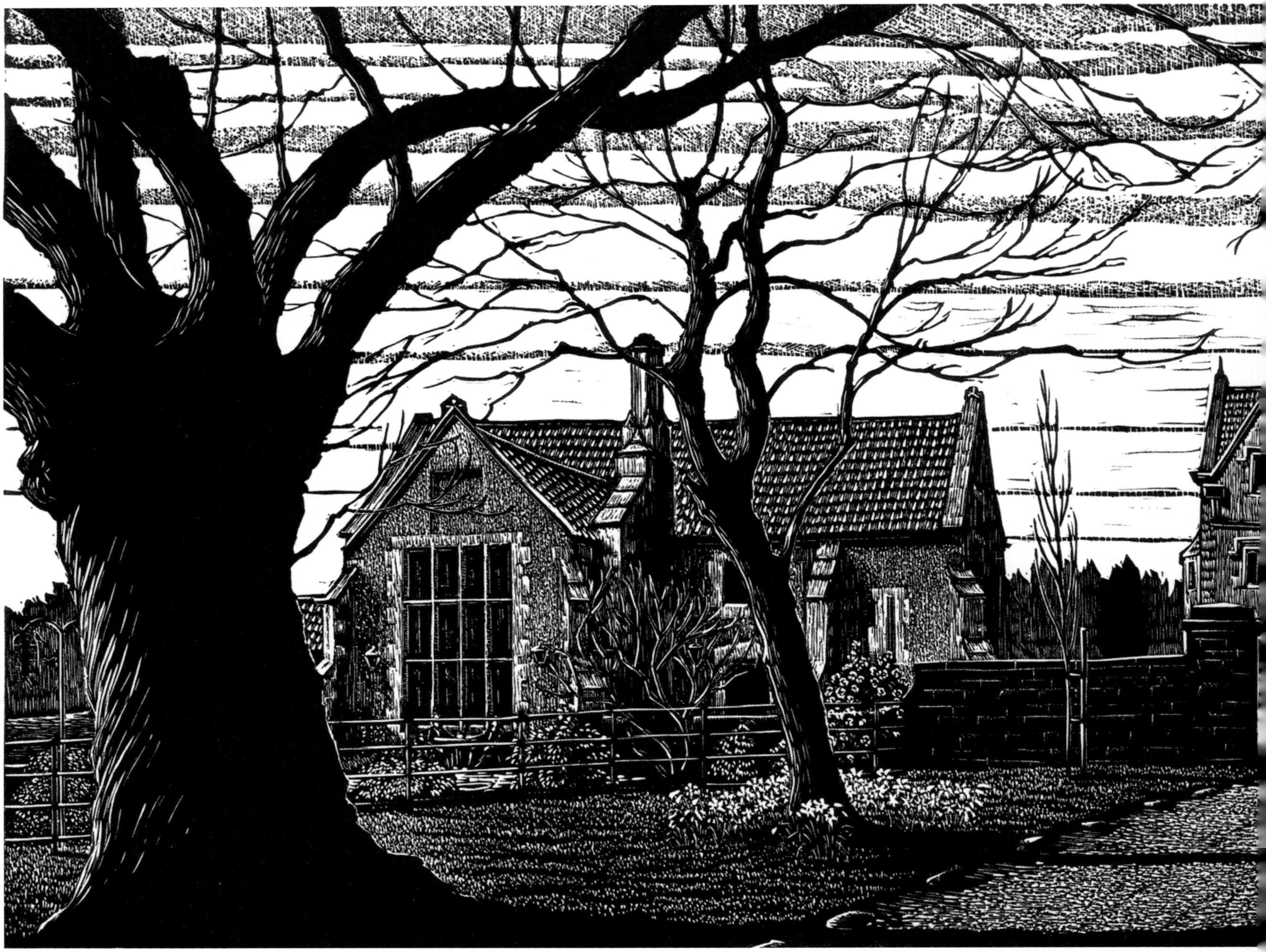

50 *Nailsea Court from the Driveway*
17 x 48 cms (7 x 18 3/4 ins)

This was commissioned in 2002 from the owners of part of the estate. It is a hidden treasure. This imposing Elizabethan house was in a ruinous state some years ago and only saved from demolition by being converted into apartments.

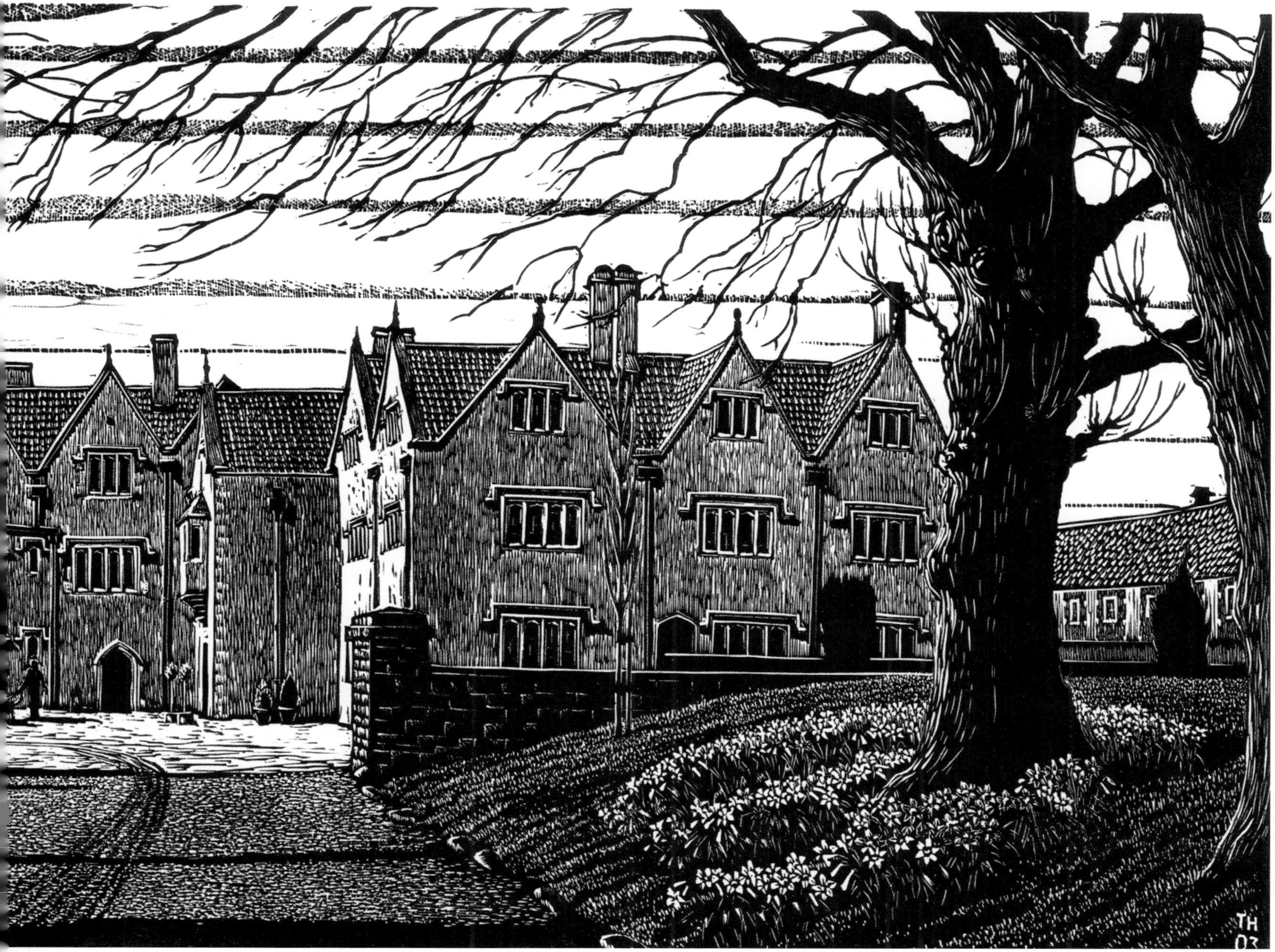
TH
03

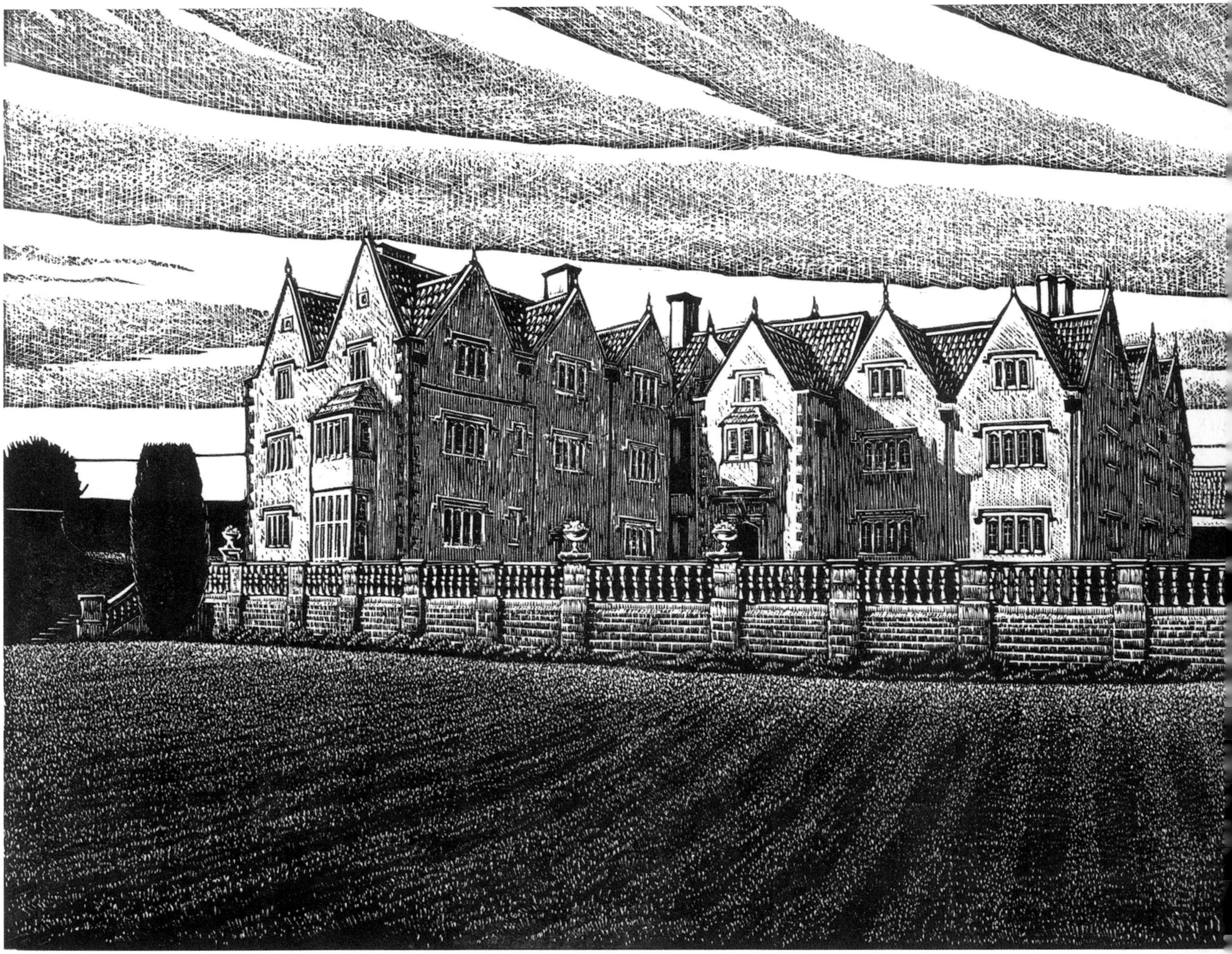

51 *Nailsea Court: the main façade*
reduced from 17 x 48cms (7 x 18 3/4 ins)

Another view from the lawn in front of the house.

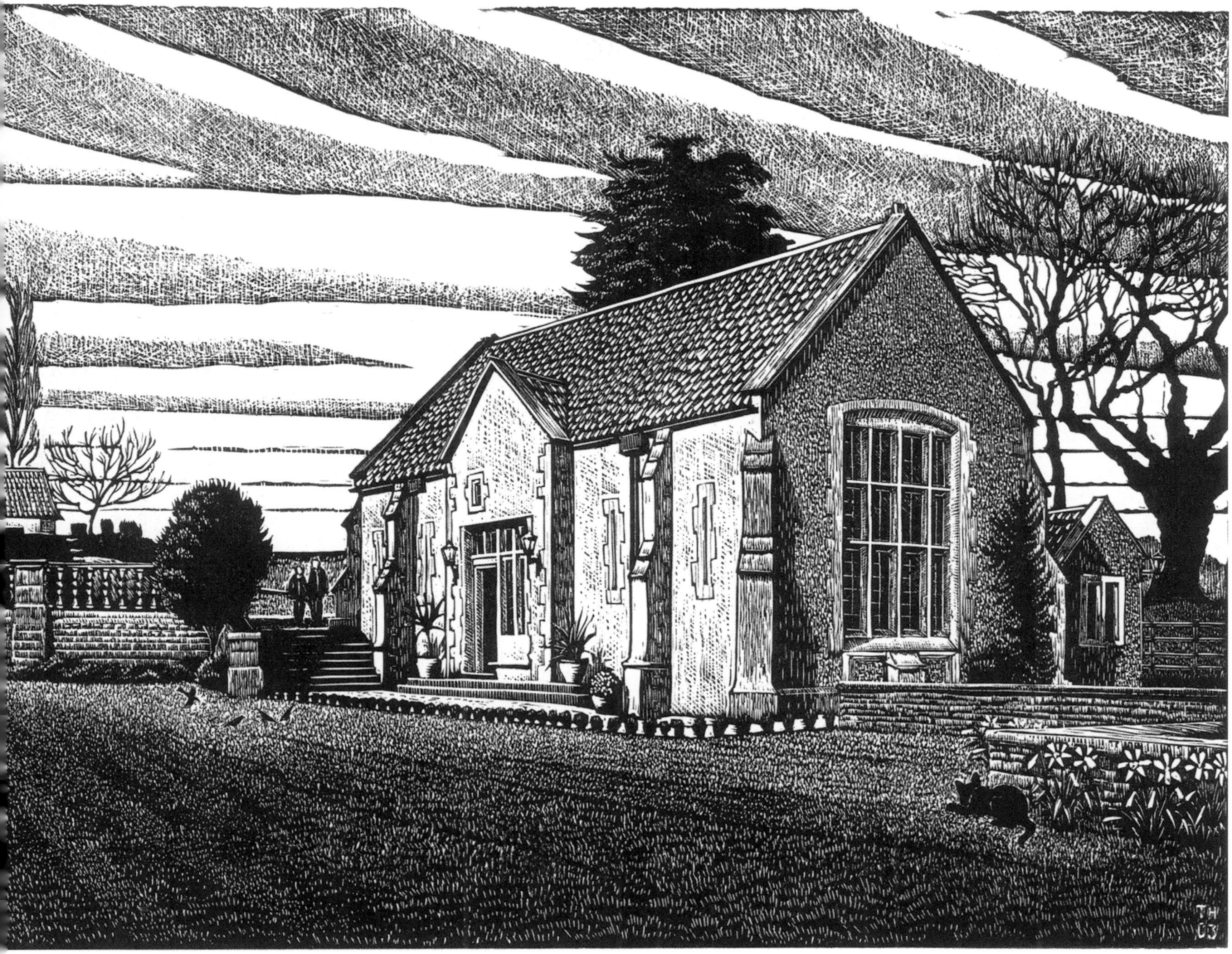
TH
03

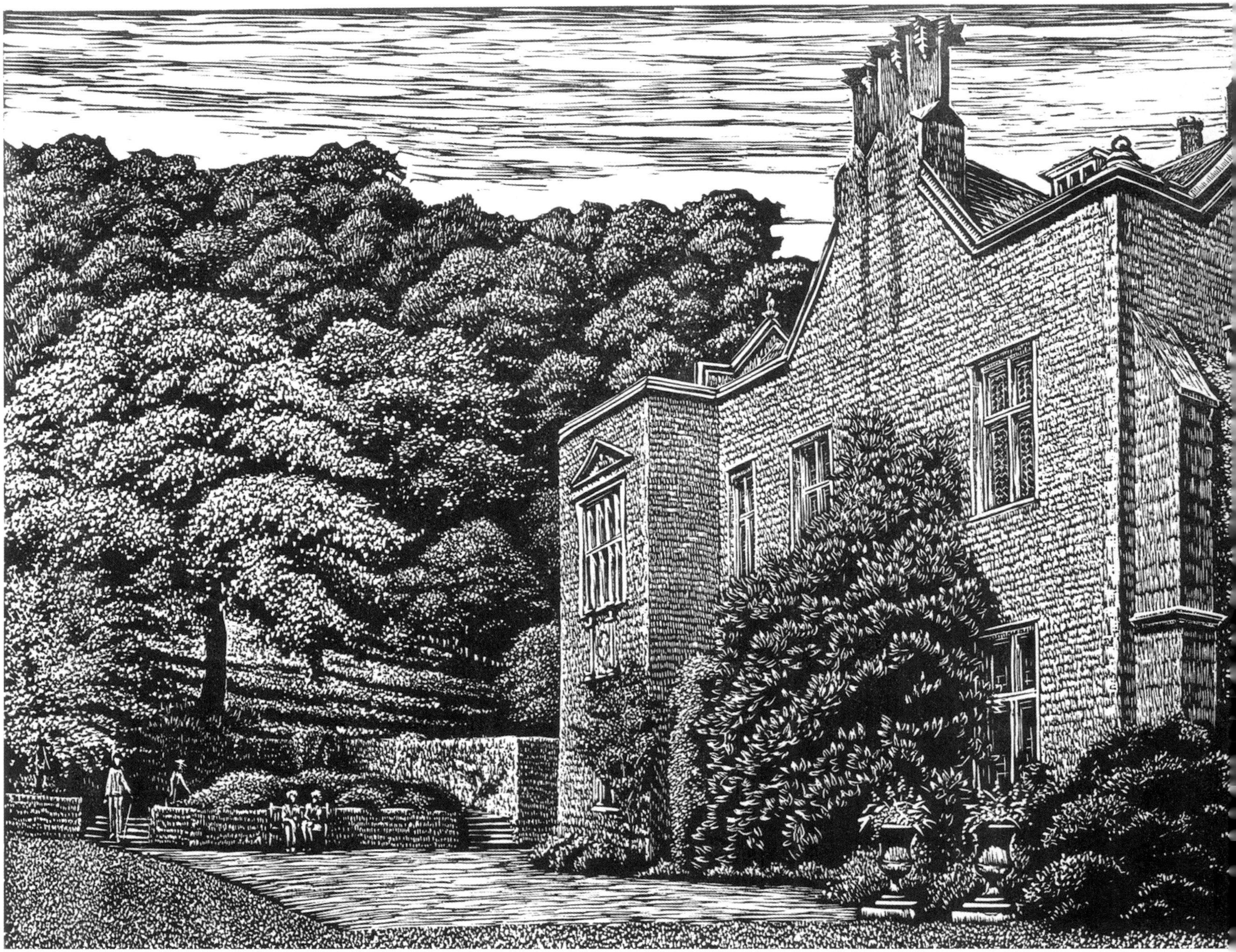

52 *Clevedon Court*

reduced from 17 x 48cms (7 x 18 3/4 ins)

This fine old house has been through many incarnations over the centuries and there are hints of all of them in what remains. This is now owned by the National Trust.

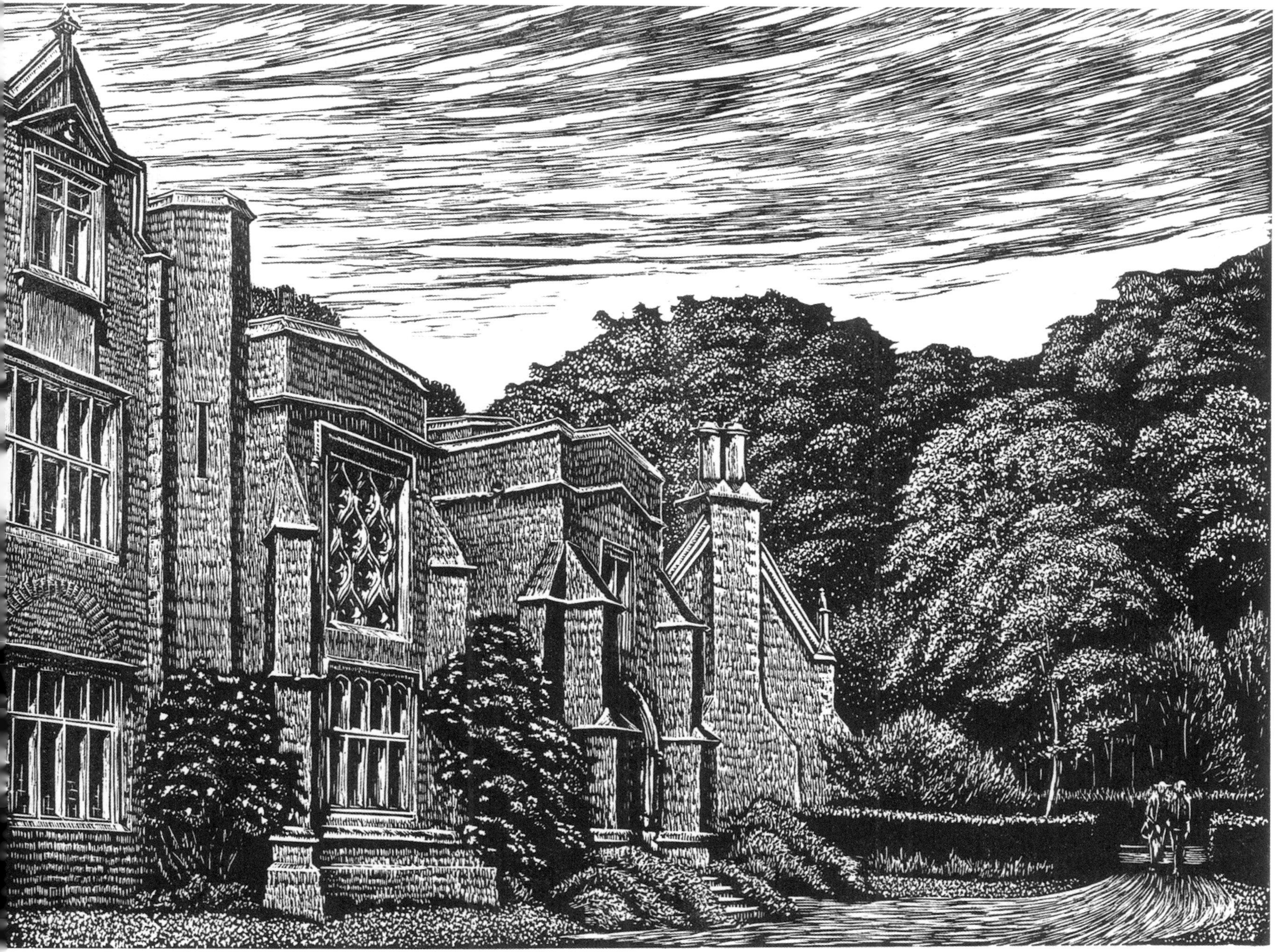

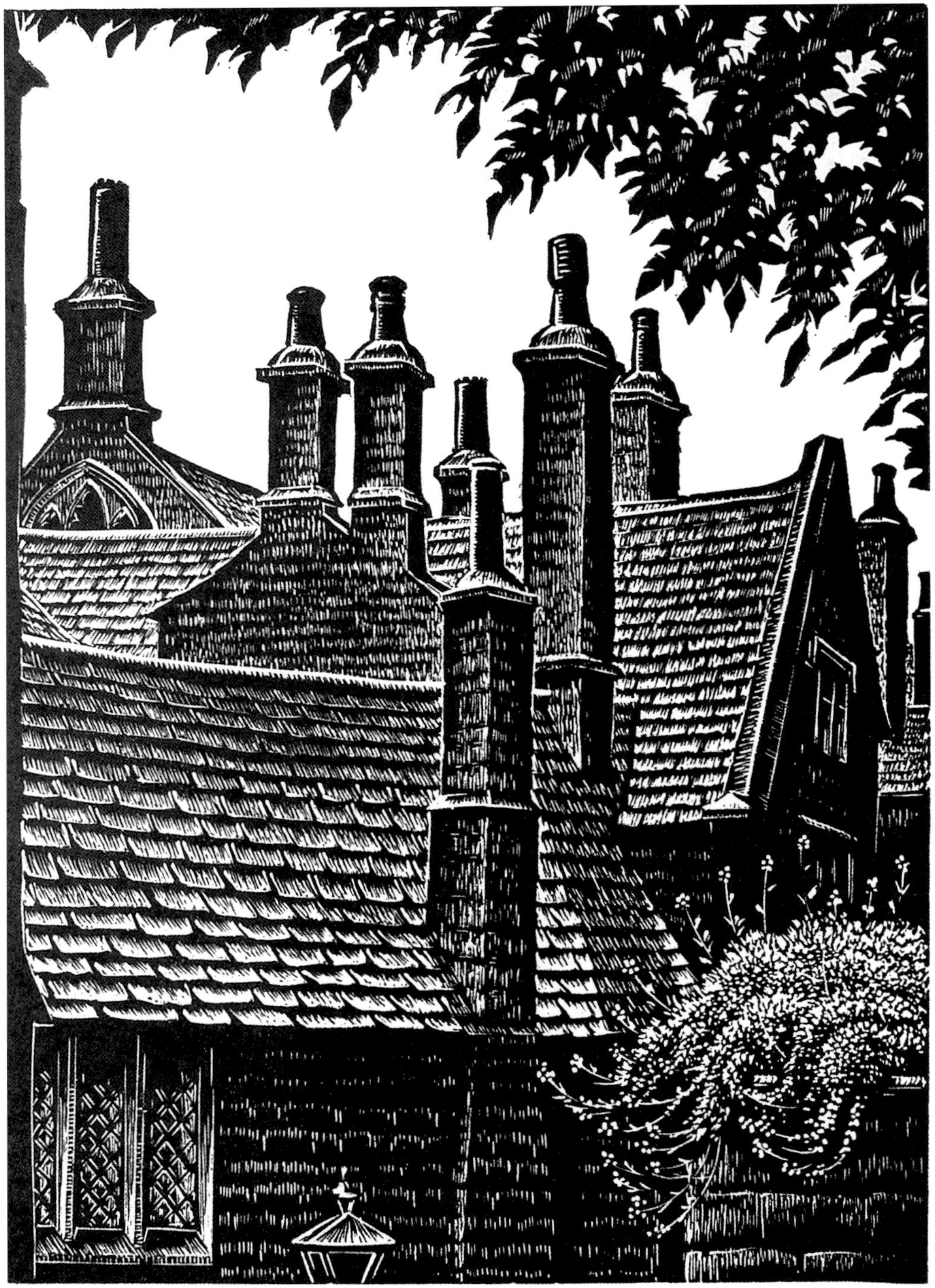

53 *Chimneys at the rear of Clevedon Court*
actual size

I'm always drawn to the sculptural qualities of roofscapes like this. I've recorded many different ones during my time as an artist, in this country and abroad.

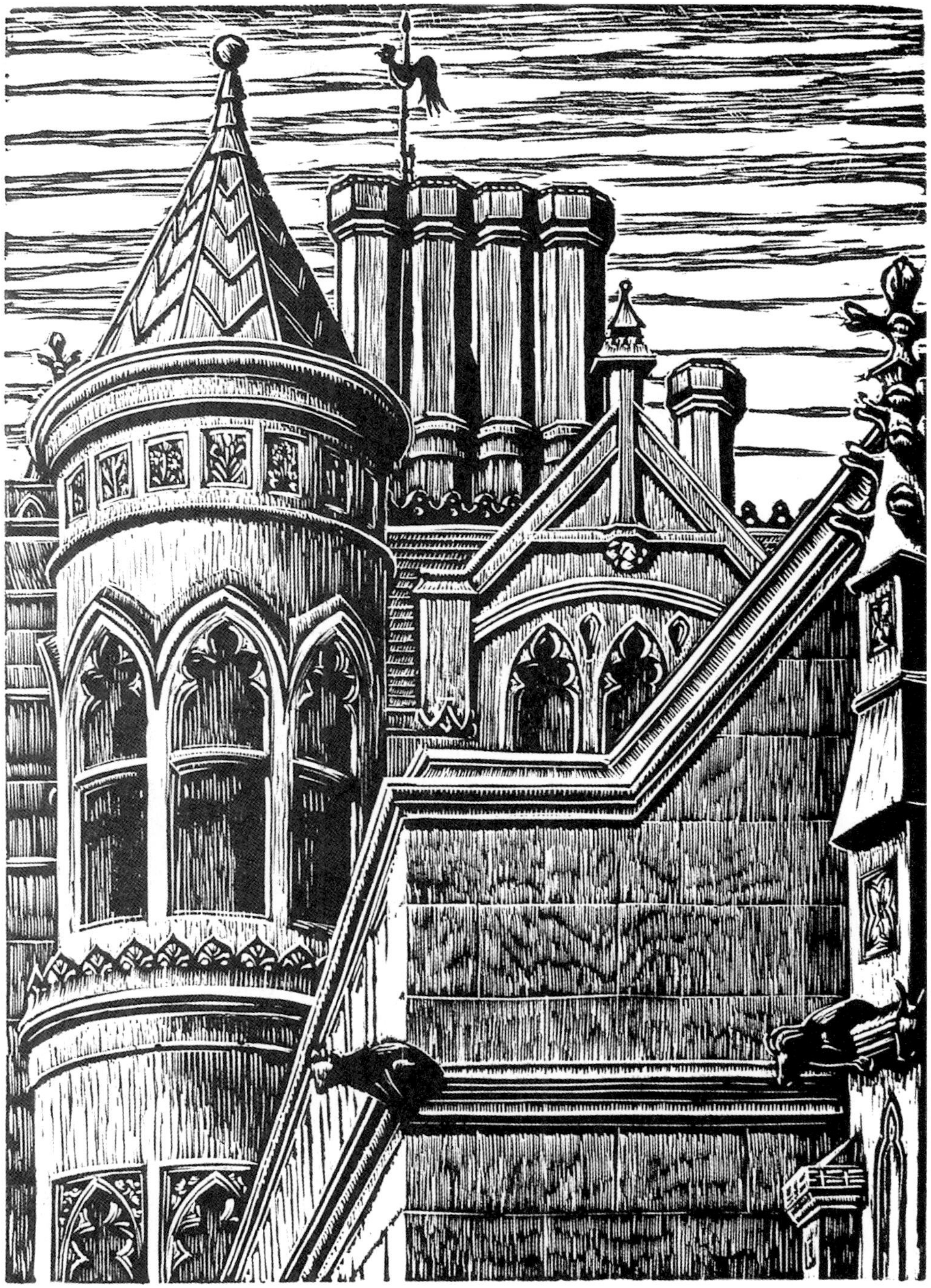

54 *Roofscape, Tyntesfield, Wraxall*
actual size

This, the former home of Lord Wraxall, was recently taken over by the National Trust. It is a fascinating place, blending high craftsmanship and fantasy in a most beguiling way.

I loved this conglomeration of ornate turrets, gable ends and chimney stacks.

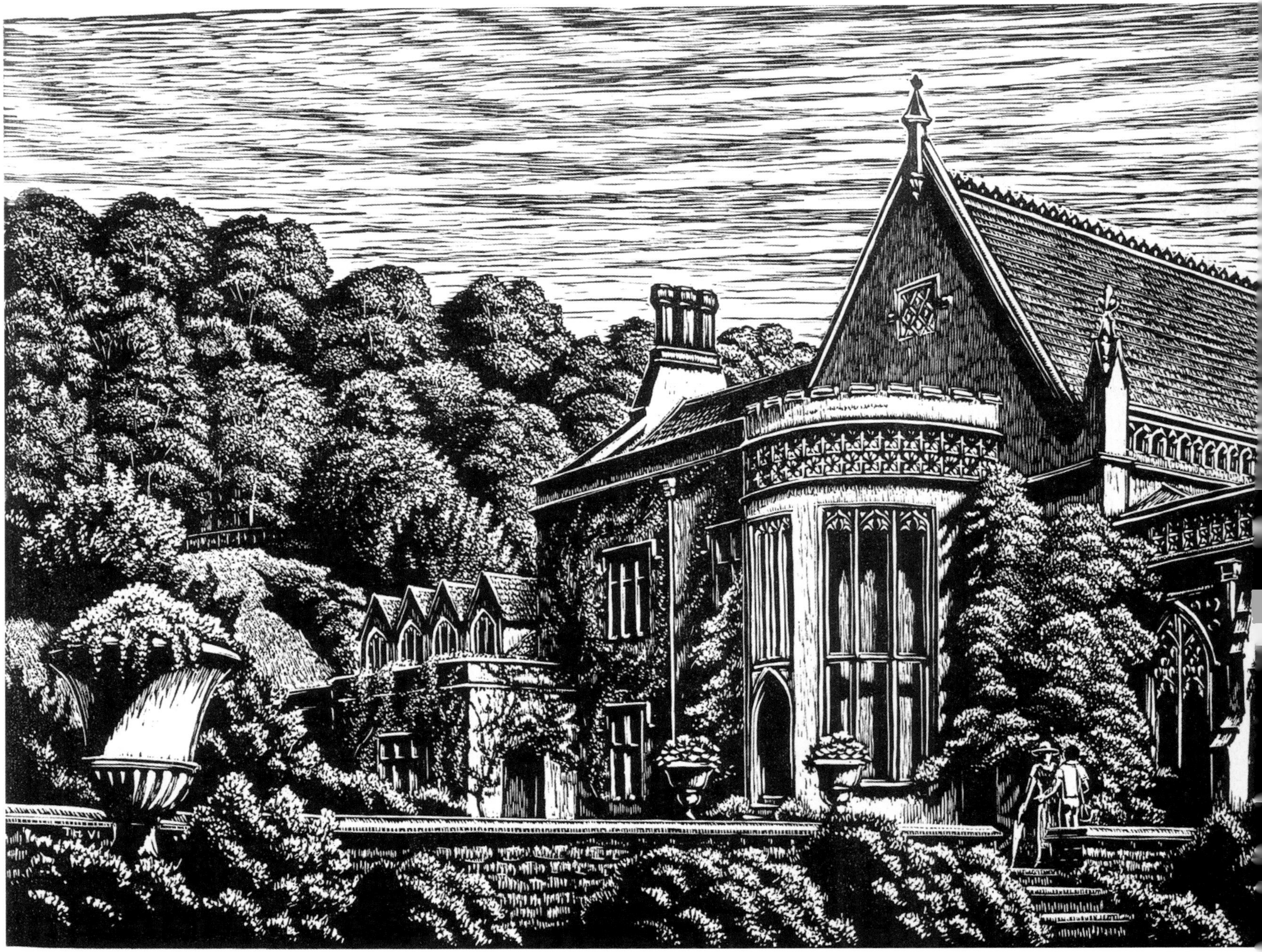

55 *Tyntesfield: the main façade*
reduced from 17 x 48cms (7 x 18¾ins)

I have visited Tyntesfield only once so far, but would like to do more work there soon.

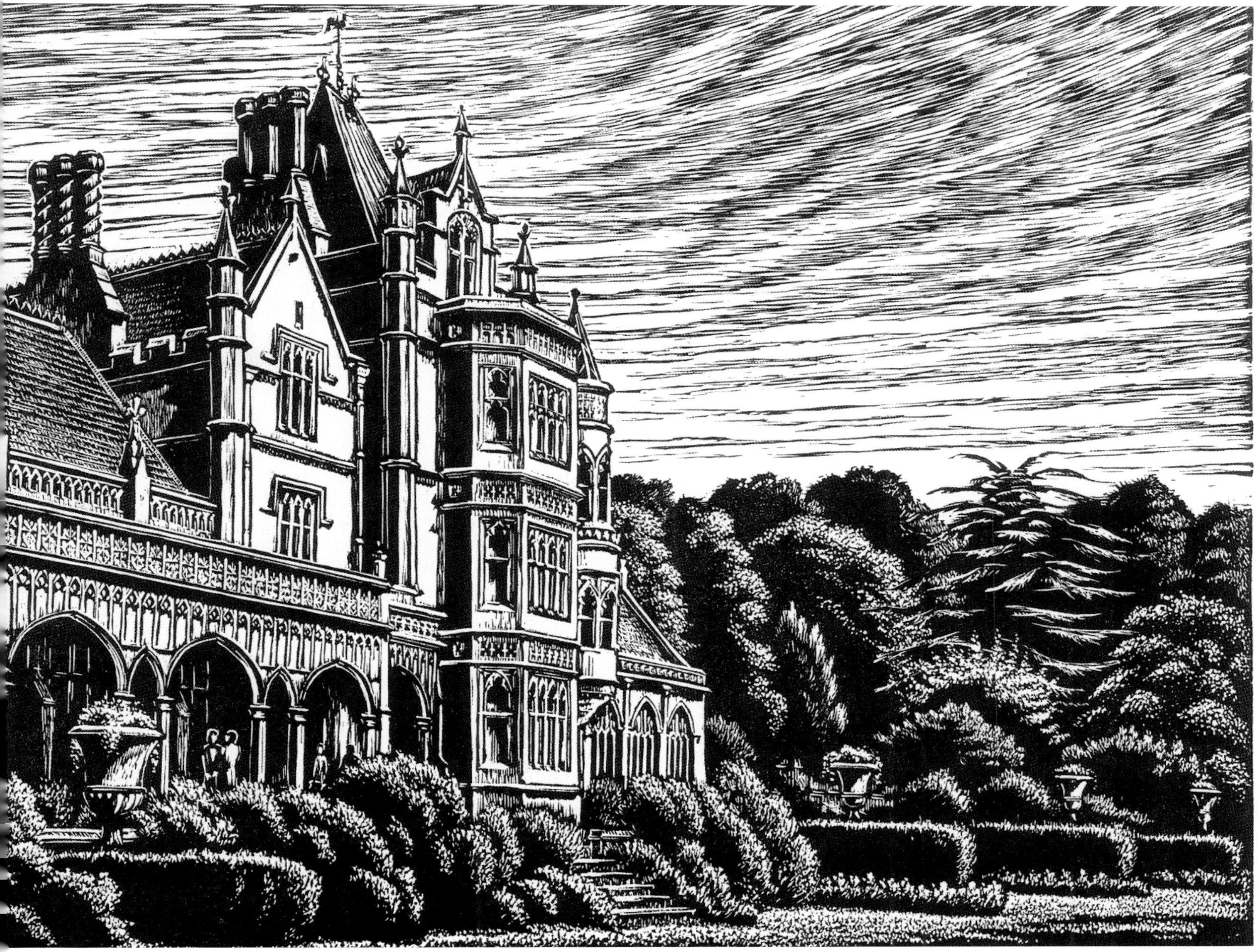

Conclusion

I hope this new collection of engravings of Bristol and its environs gives pleasure to those who see it. It's been an enjoyable experience producing them and though I've now completed just over 100 views of the city, I'm sure these won't be my last. The city offers up an endless supply of possible subjects, and I'm always amazed how one can suddenly 'see' a new composition in an entirely familiar place after years of being blind to it. This is one of the thrills of being an artist, I suppose, and what drives me on in my work.

There's certainly much yet to be done.

To quote T.S. Eliot:

> We shall not cease from exploration
> And the end of all our exploring
> Will be to arrive where we started
> And know the place for the first time
>
> ('Little Gidding', *The Four Quartets*)

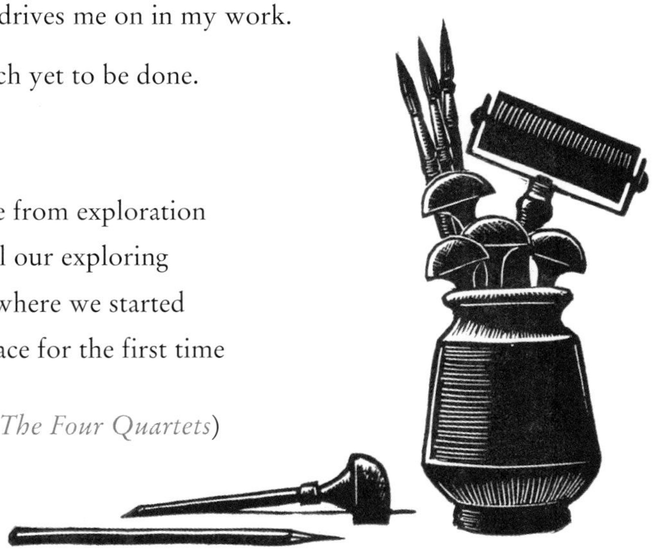

List of Engravings

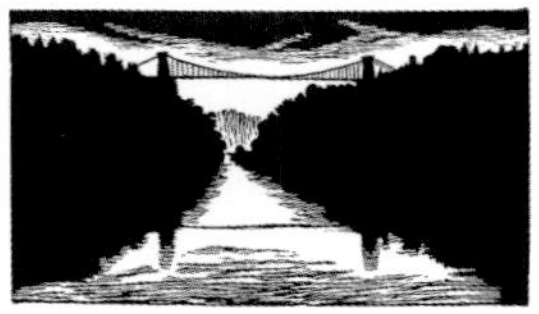

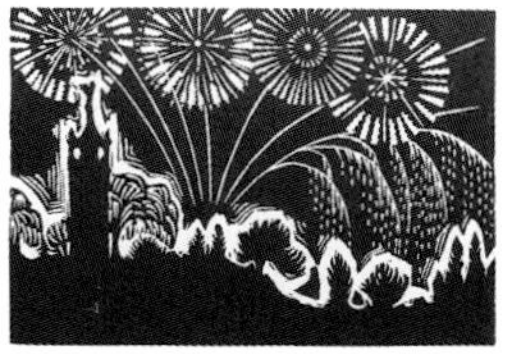

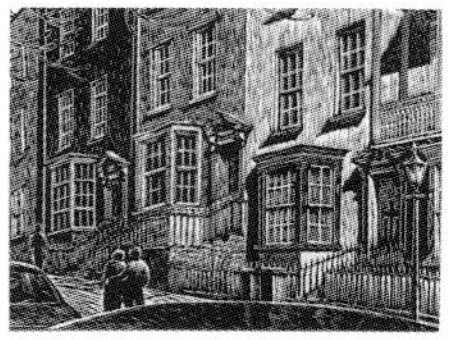

Clifton, Clifton Wood and Redland

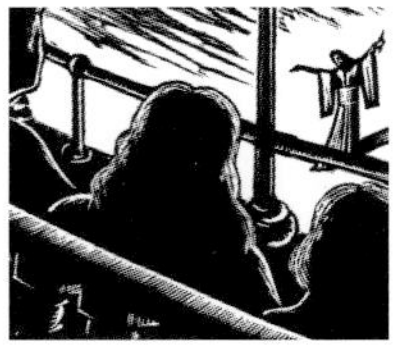

A Theatrical Interlude

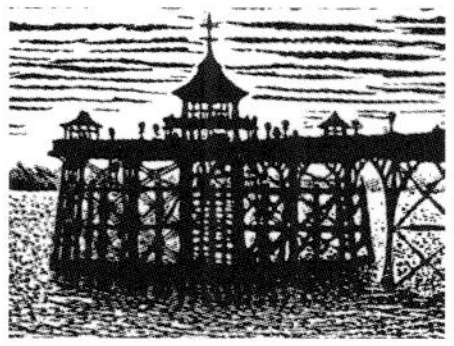

And Beyond

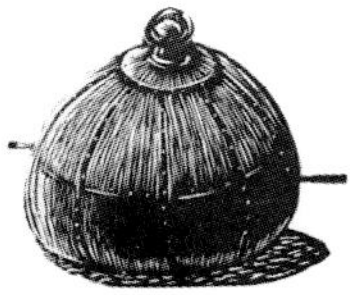

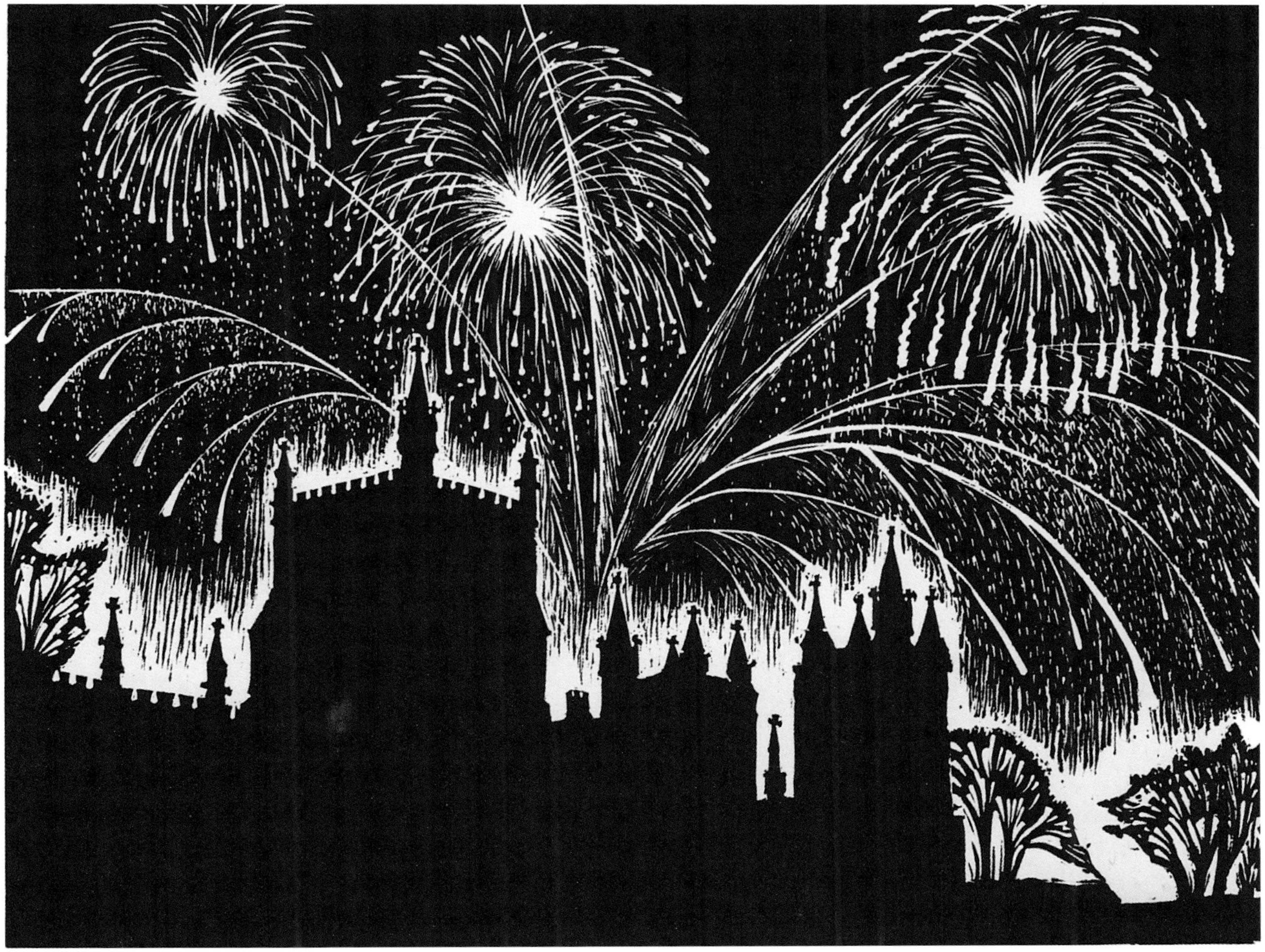

The Grand Finale: Fireworks behind Bristol Cathedral
actual size

With many thanks to John and Angela Sansom;
to my partner, John, for his helpful comments and
support thoughout the making of this book; to
my friend and artistic confidante, Rachel and to
everyone who encouraged me in this project.
I am very grateful.
Trevor Haddrell 2006

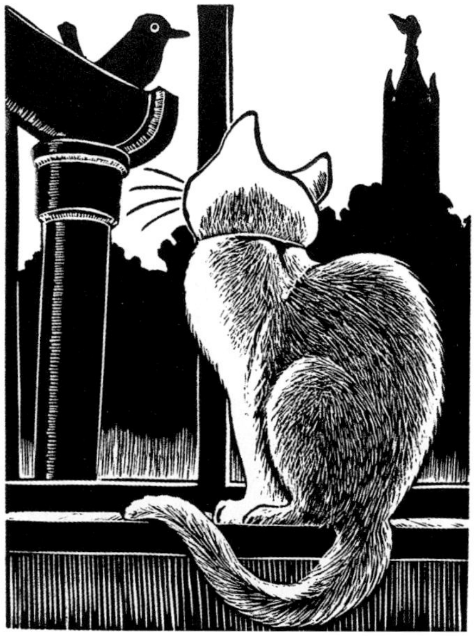